"Burden finds spiritual meaning in nooks and crannies most of us miss. From the Temple Mount to an old pew in Maine, here is a paean about paying attention.... With an eye on the birds and a heart toward heaven, Burden's *Wings over the Wall* effortlessly soars above the rest."

—Dr. Eli Knapp (Houghton College),
author of *The Delightful Horror of Family Birding*

"*Wings over the Wall* is a book for Christians who yearn for a closer walk with God. For those who appreciate sharing quests, Burden invites you into much of his life's pilgrimage. For folks who can only dream of visiting the sacred sites in the Holy Land, this book will transport you there in your imagination. For those who have been privileged to make a pilgrimage to the Holy Land, you will be reminded of what you experienced and humbled by what you missed, as I was."

—Rev. Dr. Scott Dow, owner of
Transformation Travel, LLC

D0861635

WINGS
OVER THE
WALL

Faith, Birding, and Walking with Jesus in the Holy Land

WINGS
OVER THE
WALL

Matthew Burden

North Wind Publishing
Brewer, Maine 04412

North Wind Publishing, P.O. Box 3655, Brewer, ME 04412.
http://northwindpublishing.com/

ISBN-13: 978-1-7329319-6-1

Library of Congress Control Number: 2021931169

Text and Cover Design by Janet Robbins

CONTENTS

Part 3

Through the Church the Song Goes On – Disciples, Saints, and Pilgrims

INTRODUCTION

This book is the record of a pilgrimage I took to Israel in 2018, but the book itself is a pilgrimage as well. Our tour leader, Scott, told us that his highest hope was for us to have an authentic pilgrimage experience in Israel—by which he meant not just a nice time taking pictures of very old places, but an encounter with Christ himself, as we entered the story of his life, death, and resurrection. This book is designed with the hope of opening the door for just such an experience. It won't just give you a lovely, descriptive tour of Gospel locations, though there are many uses for books like that. It will take you on the journey of walking with a fellow pilgrim through those very places, to reflect together on the path of Jesus there.

This book is a devotional memoir, in which I serve as friend and guide. I'll be pointing out some of my favorite things as we go—birds, interesting points of history, theological insights, and more birds—and I hope that, even if these things are not as interesting to you as they are to me, you will find, in my delight, an opportunity to consider them with fresh eyes.

You will also find that your guide is intent on laying bare his soul on the slightest whim. This is by design. To enter into an authentic pilgrimage experience, one needs to be honest about one's heart. If I had taken a tour just to snap a few pictures and add a few birds to my life list, it would not be a pilgrimage. Making pilgrimage is a spiritual practice, it is about more than learning, seeing, or visiting. It's about taking your whole self, body and soul, and committing to a pathway of bearing witness to what God has done, and then opening yourself up to being transformed anew by his grace. It's an ancient tradition that Jesus himself undertook, as did all pious Jews when they went up to Jerusalem for the festivals. So for this to be a pilgrimage, I have to tell you about my heart. My hope is that this will be an encouragement for you to consider your own heart's journey along the way.

I should perhaps add that my spiritual life in Christ has always felt like a journey to me, a quest that was taking me somewhere. It has been marked, in relatively equal degrees, by peace and by passion—on the one hand, the simple assurance and blessedness of knowing God's grace and walking humbly with him; on the other hand, the burning of fierce desires to go deeper, to experience and attain greater heights of the holiness he has granted, and to be of ever greater use to his glory. But as you read this book, you will likely hear a great deal more of the "passion" side than the "peace." The reason for that is simple: the opportunity to take a prayerful, intentional pilgrimage to the Holy Land, to encounter Christ in the places that were meaningful to him, had such a profound pull on me that its gravity drew all my hopes and desires up to a high tide of anticipation. All of my longings for what my walk with God ought to be like—yearnings that are present, but usually in the background, in my normal, everyday life—were drawn up to such a point that I walked the roads of Israel pierced with their sharpness. It was something of a surprise to me that I should be so deeply moved when I arrived there; I hadn't anticipated feeling the way I did. But one of the rules of pilgrimage is that you have to take yourself with you, everywhere you go, and there was no way of separating the journey of my heart from the journey of my feet.

A few more notes before we begin: there are many people far more qualified to write books about Israel than I am. I have my own expertise in history, theology, and birding that I will bring to bear on the topic, but this book is not meant to be a full picture of the complex realities of the Holy Land. My experience there was brief, and this is a book about those few days, and those days alone. Pilgrimage tours are sometimes criticized for avoiding the hard truths about what daily life in Israel and the West Bank is really like, and I freely acknowledge that my book does not have a great deal to say on the matter. I did my best to read as many sources as I could on the culture, history, and current affairs of Israel's peoples before I went on my trip, and that was tremendously useful during my time there. One of my hopes for this book is that it will inspire readers to learn more, perhaps to go and see for themselves, and to fill out my incomplete picture with an experience of Israel that is fuller and richer in the end.

This book is arranged in short chapters, each recounting a site or two that we visited, and connecting the places with some devotional and theological reflections. There are three main parts to the book, with the large middle section serving as the core of the narrative. The first few chapters (Part 1) relate to my personal experience of getting to Israel, and then the majority of the book (Part 2) walks sequentially through the story of Jesus, beginning with the annunciation in Nazareth, before wrapping up with a few closing reflections on the early church and my return journey home (Part 3). My tour group did not visit the sites in the order laid out in these pages, but I chose to offer a more coherent narrative by following the pathway of Jesus' story rather than the pinball movements of our group's itinerary. The names of some people in the story have been changed, specifically those whom I could not contact to obtain their consent for appearing in this book.

Special thanks go to Transformation Travel LLC and to its founder, Scott Dow, who was a fellow pilgrim on our journey. I'm especially grateful for the thoughtful, intentional way his tours are put together, and for his flexibility and cheerfulness during all phases of planning and implementing our trip. Another major figure in the story of Transformation Travel is Rev. Dr. Ken Parker, whose work in designing a profoundly devotional model of pilgrimage enriched the experience more than I can say. Thanks also to my brother, Josh, one of the organizers of the trip and a man I am proud to call both a friend and a fellow worker in the ministry. His companionship made the whole experience brighter, and his organizational skill kept everything running smoothly throughout. His theological insight and advice also played a large role in finalizing this manuscript for publication, and I'm deeply grateful to him for that. Further thanks to all my other fellow pilgrims, whose kind fellowship wove strength and joy throughout the experience. I'm also tremendously grateful for the support, prayers, and funding offered by my church family at Second Baptist Church of Calais, Maine, without which none of this would have been possible, and whose labors for the Lord bless and uphold me. And finally, highest thanks to my wife, Rachel, who made the great sacrifice of letting me go off adventuring while she stayed home with our three kids. Her love, graciousness, and joy are my greatest inspiration.

Part 1

"Just a Closer Walk with Thee"
My Journey to Israel

THE WAY OF A PILGRIM

By the grace of God I am a Christian,
By my works a great sinner,
And by calling a humble wanderer,
Roaming from place to place.

—Anonymous nineteenth-century Russian author

I had fairly low expectations of my pilgrimage to the Holy Land, except that I was hoping it would change my life forever.

The truth is, I was well aware that my glimpse of Israel would be far from a complete picture. I knew I would be shown a tour of the country presented in snapshots of carefully curated locations, interspersed with air-conditioned rides that would take me past many of the tensions and fractures of daily life. I knew that some of the presented sites would lean on historical conjectures that amounted to wishful thinking. And I knew that eight days was a laughably small window in which to claim an understanding of that part of the world; still less to pretend that I, in my brief bus-window experience, could say I had some association with it.

And yet I felt, every now and then, an edge of anticipation flashing its vibrant plumage in quick and brilliant flyovers in my mind. I imagined myself standing beneath the great rotunda in the Church of the Holy Sepulchre, the place where history changed forever—the place where I had changed forever—when Jesus rose from the tomb in triumph over sin, death, and hell. And when I imagined that, my vision swam with tears. I wasn't sure why. I knew I didn't have to go there to be a good Christian, nor to understand and appreciate the death and resurrection of Christ. But I also knew, deeply and intuitively, that if I were there, it would set the deepest chords of my heart in resonant motion.

Though I would like to present myself as a casual and disinterested observer of the biblical landscape, like a gentleman-adventurer of the Victorian era, who measured and appreciated the experience in perfect moderation, subject to the regal dignity and discipline of his own well-molded character...I can't. I just can't. You see, when I began to think about going on pilgrimage, I suddenly felt the swell of a great unspoken desire rising like a tide within me: the longing to be transformed. I wanted the journey to change me irrevocably, to make me a man of disciplined godliness, a man who not only wanted to be good but who was consistently able to bring that desire to completion in his behavior. But that wasn't me. I didn't have it all together. I wanted to go and meet with Jesus on the shores of Galilee, but I knew that I wasn't going as the righteous, but as a sinner.

And perhaps that's as it should be.

———·———

In ancient days, pilgrimage was all about the journey. Whether by land or sea, in every era except the past century, getting to the Holy Land took weeks of travel, if not months. Because of the rigors of the road, pilgrimage became a self-imposed course of spiritual discipline: prayers for safety, the fasting of having only travel provisions to eat, and the bodily mortification of long days on foot. By the time pilgrims reached the Holy Land, they had already been formed by their long march into the depth and peace of discipline. The holy sites then became the rich reward of a prize long sought, for which ample room had already been made in their hearts.

We modern pilgrims are not so lucky. While there's much to be said for the efficiency and convenience of air travel, it bears with it the temptation to turn pilgrimages into mere tourist trips. Instead of the soul-shaping rigors of a walk across nations or a voyage over uncertain waves, we instead spend a day in the awkward no-man's-land of buses, terminals, and airplane seats. What I'm trying to say, by way of my Luddite complaints, is that the actual journey of getting to the Holy Land didn't feel real. When we stepped into the air of Israel, it seemed as though we had simply gone through an odd transmigration to a different world altogether.

But I need to back up a bit and tell you a little about that journey—the road that brought me to the Holy Land. In many ways, it was not altogether unlike the road that I had walked with Christ for many years. So, since the story of my travels to get to Israel are not really all that interesting, I'll tell you the real story of my pilgrimage, the paths of my heart that brought me to that point. Because, you see, we are all on pilgrimage, whether we know it or not.

LEAVING HOME

But my one unchanged obsession,
Wheresoe'er my feet have trod,
Is a keen, enormous, haunting,
Never-sated thirst for God.

—Adapted from Gamaliel Bradford's poem *"God"*

My pilgrimage began when I said yes. That's the way all pilgrimages begin, including the most important: our journey into the love and knowledge of God. I said yes to this experience, not because I thought I needed it, but for a host of other reasons: my brother invited me to come; I liked to travel and to see other countries; I would be able to rack up some new sightings for my birding life list; I had an interest in the historical background of the area; and, more than anything else, there was that waning spark of a hope that perhaps, just perhaps, God might someday give me a fresh experience of his grace that would bring long-sought-for peace in the struggle to walk in holiness.

My brother, Josh, was the one who invited me. He was one of the tour "hosts," wearing multiple hats as a recruiter, organizer, and pastor for our little group. The journey began for me on a chill April morning in Maine. It was the feast day of William Law, whose compelling masterpiece, *A Serious Call to a Devout and Holy Life,* I had spent the previous year in reading. The day was bright but cold, and I left the house early. The plan was to drive two hours to the bus station, and then ride another four hours to the airport, where I would meet the rest of the team and embark on our overnight flight to Tel Aviv. And that plan played out with perfect, almost boring precision. But, truth be told, boring is kind of what one wants when it comes to the logistics of modern travel.

Public buses had been my regular form of travel when I was a young man, going back and forth between home and college and my future wife's house in Pennsylvania, so the old routine came back to me with quiet homeliness: the smooth paper of the tickets, my suitcase getting placed in the undercarriage, and the feeling of settling into an uncomfortable seat and watching the haggard, post-winter forests of Maine slip past the windows.

———·———

My journey of faith had been comfortably familiar, too, for most of my life. I was raised in a missionary family, first in Brazil and then at home in Maine, and all my young memories were suffused with a joyful adherence to the Christian way of life. My relationship with Jesus was, in equal measures, thrilling and deeply peaceful. I had some stirring adventures along the way, like doing undercover ministry as a young man, living in an Islamist-ruled North African country. I also had many soul-filling moments of deep and intimate connection with God, mountaintop experiences of worship, prayer, and spiritual consolation. I was alight with faith's fire, from the child who joined the church prayer meeting to learn intercession from prayer warriors six decades older, to the young adult who traveled land-mine-infested roads to minister in distant backwaters of the African bush. But what I didn't really understand at the time was that the journey of Christian pilgrimage could bring with it not only the rising road of spiritual consolation, but the dark night of desolation as well.

———·———

My bus to the airport was rolling ever closer to the city. I can recall seeing the unbroken, mind-numbing dystopia of modern urban life scroll by in an endless succession of stoplights and merges as we approached the airport, and I longed for my Maine forests again, chill and leafless though they were. As if to complete the feeling of urban desolation, it began to rain as we rode the ramps up to the international terminal: gray skies above, and slick wet concrete below. I suddenly felt the overwhelming call of the primitivist, the clarion bellow of Thoreau somewhere deep in the recesses of my mind, telling me that this world of gray metropolises and mechanized technology would suck my soul with cold vampiric sadism until I had no humanity left. (It may be that I'm not really a "city person.")

The roots of my season of desolation ran deep, far deeper than I cared to admit to myself during my younger days. One of the unchanging markers of my spiritual life has been an agonizing awareness of my own sinfulness. That's not necessarily a bad thing, especially in the Western Christian tradition, since this sense of conviction and compunction leads one to repentance and deeper reliance on the grace of God. And I was grateful for God's grace, truly I was— I had no doubts that his grace was effective, that my sins were atoned for, that the record of my wrongs was covered over in the righteousness of Christ. But where God's grace was infinite, I could muster only the sparsest grace for myself. I knew I could be better, and I knew I should be better, and as a result, I was unflinching in my self-reproach. I had stumbled into what Dallas Willard calls "the gospel of sin management." I became perpetually frustrated with myself for my inability to make progress toward a perfectly holy way of life, despite all the empowering blessings the Holy Spirit had given me.

When I was fourteen years old, I read *Byzantium*, a novel by Stephen Lawhead—the story of a medieval monk and his travels. I became entranced with the notion of monasticism: an ordered, highly disciplined Christian life, centered on the pursuit of personal holiness. Though, as a Baptist, I had no real-life knowledge of monastic practice, the idea became an ideal in my young mind. I began to learn the stories of great monks of the past, like Antony and Benedict, and yearned to be able to emulate their ascetic discipline in my own life.

But I was a young man, living at the turn of the millennium in the secularizing, temptation-drenched culture of modern America, and I was poignantly aware of every failing and every stumble along my way. The everyday sins of youth—lust, gluttony, pride, and a host of others—I felt as daggers in my soul, and I didn't know why I couldn't simply be rid of them, and live the rigorous, ascetic, holy life I wanted to live. I thought I ought to have enough willpower to just transform myself from the inside out, to be who I wanted to be, but the sin-tainted frailty of my human nature kept rising to make itself known, over and over and over again.

There are a few Protestant traditions that believe God grants a sort of second stage in the Christian life, a moment of entire sanctification, in which these struggles against sin end (at least for the most part), to be replaced with a daily tally of triumphant spiritual victories. That wasn't the teaching I grew up with, but I was familiar with it. I hoped it was true, but I doubted it—it didn't seem to match my personal experience, nor that of most Christians I knew. The truth is, I suspect that God, in the mystery of his providence, may work that way with some people, here and there granting a dramatic surge of practical holiness; but I haven't observed it to be a general rule, either in biblical evidence or the actual experience of my fellow Christians. So I wasn't really expecting a lightning bolt from the blue to instantaneously make me the greatest saint the world had ever seen; I was just hoping to see some consistent progress in walking the road of self-disciplined growth as portrayed in the New Testament's vision of Christian living. And yet those steps of progress seemed few and far between, with a great many slips and stumbles along the way.

My frustrations with myself also left me with many unanswered questions for God. Why didn't he help me? Why didn't he deliver me? What possible reason could he have for not answering my prayers? Did he want me to be stuck forever in this slate-gray world of holy longings and dashed hopes?

It was during this season of my life that the experiential part of my interior life of faith died away completely. Not that I let it die—rather, it was taken away. It felt like a hideous betrayal. My walk with God had always had a strongly experiential element to it—I could feel his presence with me, sometimes so powerfully that it was overwhelming. And all of the sudden, in the period of my deepest desperation, that sense of his presence was ripped away from me. It didn't feel like I had pushed God away with my questions or frustrations; if anything, I had been praying and reaching out to him much more earnestly than ever before. And that was the moment he chose to leave. It was as if a toddler, crying out for his daddy's embrace, suddenly had his father snatch away his blanket, walk out of the room, and close the door behind him.

This loss of the presence of God felt incomprehensible. I wasn't really aware at the time of the long tradition of Christian experience that understood such seasons to be a natural and necessary part of growing in faith, that I was facing an invitation to a hard but higher road, where I could be weaned from my accustomed consolations in order to know God even more fully. It wasn't until later that I would come to realize that what had happened to me was almost exactly the experience that Gregory of Nyssa, in the fourth century, described in terms of entering the darkness of the unknowability of God, or that John of the Cross wrote about in the sixteenth century, speaking of "the dark night of the soul."

I wandered through a few years of heart-wrenching disillusionment and doubt. Those doubts took seriously the intellectual challenges to Christianity, but they weren't the primary driver. I knew the arguments of atheists very well, and had studied them more closely than most, but they seldom struck me as deeply convincing. I read the most thorough books I could find on both sides of the argument for God's existence, and was lucky enough to have a brother willing to engage in months upon months of wandering dialogues. If anything, even amid my darkest doubts, it was the evidence of physics, cosmology, and classic philosophy that kept me from ever being able to renounce a belief in God. So I clung to a yearning, desperate hope that he was there, but with a brokenhearted bewilderment at his abandonment. Like riding that bus through a gray, beleaguered world, I was just holding on to the hope that around some distant corner up ahead, I might finally arrive at where I was longing to be.

And just like that bus ride, I did come out of the land of gray skies and into the brilliance and warmth of a whole new place. God, in his mercy, brought me out of my dark night of the soul (I'll tell the story of that experience a bit later on). My faith was confirmed, my doubts assuaged, and my heart restored to the peace of knowing that God was with me on my journey. Many Christians are afraid to walk roads of doubt, and are far too quick to attack such journeys in others' lives. It's too often viewed as a lack of faith, a selfish apostasy, a problem to be solved. In my case, though—and I suspect in the case of more than a few others as well—I came out into a deeper Christian maturity than I had ever had before, and which I don't believe would have been possible without going through the darkness.

But even that change, as wonderful as it was, did not represent the full transfiguration of my spiritual life that I had hoped for as a young man. I wanted to know that I was, at the very least, making progress down the road of godly discipline. I still carried in my heart an aching desire for holiness, a piercing sense of my failings to be who I wanted to be, and a lingering, haunting awareness of the distance between myself and God. I was thirsting beyond measure to be drawn into the holy fire of union with God—what the Eastern Christian traditions call *theosis*—and I was poignantly aware of just how far away from that goal I still was.

The international terminal at the airport was a pleasant environment. It was bright and expansive, a long, soaring room paneled in the warmth of wood tones and with the vivid colors of a hundred different flags hanging overhead. A moment's glance at that panoply of nations, and I spied it: the bold white banner with solid blue lines, and in the center the sharp, six-pointed star of the ancient king. Israel seemed suddenly close.

I was the first of my group to arrive, so early that the check-in counter for El Al, the Israeli airline, had not yet opened. So I walked about and waited, and little by little the rest of our crew trickled in as other buses and planes arrived. We were eleven in all, nearly every one of us a Baptist from Maine, led by my brother, Josh, as our tour host and pastor, and Scott Dow, the organizer of the trip and owner of Transformation Travel. It was evident from the outset that we would get along well: all were pleasant, thoughtful, and full of high expectations for our trip together. Josh wasn't the only family there with me, either: my Aunt Janice had also signed on, so I was in familiar company from the beginning.

There we were, eleven travelers in a sea of luggage. Josh, true to his spartan and abstemious nature, had just a single bag that nearly would have passed as hand baggage. The rest of us had packed as one would expect of twenty-first-century Americans; my bags were heavy with the books, binoculars, and camera equipment that would serve as the indispensable tools of my journey (birding comes with its burdens, after all). We were a far cry from that first band of Christian wayfarers, sent out by the Lord with a command to take neither bag, nor staff, nor cloak. Where they had trusted in the Lord for their needs, we had suitcases so large as to preclude even the possibility of travel by foot. Nonetheless, the same hope burned bright in our hearts as in theirs:

we were disciples of the Lord, impelled by the great desire of bearing witness to the glory of his Kingdom.

Our plane took to the air, up from Boston and in a wide arc over Maine before crossing the North Atlantic and cutting over Europe. I thought of my family as we flew over the dark outline of Maine's Bold Coast far below. I already missed my wife and wished I had the sweet leaven of her presence to lighten the solitude in which I always walked, even when among friends. My kids I loved and prayed for, but I hadn't really missed them yet, not at that point. (Anyone with small children will understand.) A bit later in the trip, though, I would be longing for their bright smiles and round cheeks, and hoping against hope that one of my fellow travelers would ask about my family so that I could show off their pictures. But I did have my brother with me, and though it had been many years since we had undertaken an adventure together, it was good to be beside the old compatriot of my younger days again.

My first glimpse of the Holy Land came the next morning—or rather, thanks to the magic of time zones, the next afternoon, as we folded up our breakfast trays and started our descent. Unlike Egeria of old, who first beheld the Judean Hills from her march up through the deserts, or Richard the Lionheart, who saw the long, low coastline over the waves of the Mediterranean Sea, I saw the Holy Land like an eagle from the sky. The sea gave way to coast in a smooth and sudden line, as much unlike the jagged headlands of Maine as could be imagined. Then circling and soaring, we were over the Plain of Sharon, golden and verdant green in broad patches of cultivation. We circled down toward the airport, with just a glimpse here and there of the shining towers of Tel Aviv on the western horizon. Our wheels touched the ground, and there we were: in the Holy Land, having descended from the skies like an angel on Jacob's ladder.

ARRIVING IN ISRAEL

It may indeed be fantasy when I
Essay to draw from all created things
Deep, heartfelt, inward joy that closely clings;
And trace in leaves and flowers that round me lie
Lessons of love and earnest piety.
So let it be ... and [God] shalt not despise
Even me, the priest of this poor sacrifice.

—Samuel Taylor Coleridge, "To Nature"

My first few minutes in Israel were all about birds. After we had maneuvered through the passport and customs lines, we met our guide, an Israeli woman named Norah, and stepped out onto the curb outside the doors of Ben Gurion International Airport. It was bright and warm and reminded me of the time I had spent in Africa more than a decade before. A silvery little bus was waiting for us by the curb, and behind it a row of flowering bushes brightened the concrete pillars of the arrivals lane.

But the first thing my eyes went to, naturally, were the birds. I was three seconds in the Holy Land, and had already seen three new species: zipping over the concrete barrier, the unmistakable flash of a Red-rumped Swallow; and there, flying over the pillars, the familiar shape of a corvid, but with a striking gray cloak slung about its shoulders—a Hooded Crow; and then a flurry of motion as three yellow-gilded, starling-esque birds danced around the tires of a row of parked trucks—Common Mynas. I had pored over my field guide of Middle Eastern birds and had researched the most likely sightings at each location of our trip, but I had set fairly modest expectations. I knew that all my birding would have to be done "on the fly" as it were, in and around the planned activities of the tour; and with that constraint in place, I was thinking that I could hope to identify about twenty new species, and I would be very happy to get thirty. But this initial burst of birds, the very second I stepped out of the terminal, gave me an inkling that I might have set my hopes a bit too low.

Those who are not birders will perhaps not appreciate the sheer excitement and delight of a moment like this, but it is powerful and exhilarating. It feels like receiving wave after wave after wave of unexpected and unmerited grace. Each new bird is a marvel of God's creation, and in each one I get to share his joy in his handiwork all over again. I often feel, in my birding experiences, that I can taste just the slightest edge of the infinite delight that God felt in Genesis, chapter 1, when he looked over these creatures he had made and saw that they were good.

While the bus pulled away from the airport, we were introduced to our guide and driver via a microphone system onboard. Norah, a middle-aged Israeli woman, had a sharply intelligent gaze and a pleasant, rambling frankness in the way she talked. Our driver, Najji, knew a bit of English, but was a striking contrast to Norah's loquacity. He looked to be in his thirties, and he had a bright smile that carried winsome hints of shyness. He was a Palestinian who had grown up in Jerusalem, and it quickly became evident what an asset it would be to have our two closest companions come from both the Jewish and Palestinian communities.

Our first stop, a short drive from Ben Gurion Airport, was the old city of Jaffa (Joppa). Its brown buildings, structures that date back to the glory days of the Ottoman Empire, clustered on a prominent hill that overlooks the Mediterranean Sea. The aspect of the town, however, had probably not changed much in the past three millennia of its existence. It was easy to imagine the prophet Jonah slinking down the narrow streets toward the quay, hoping to avoid the watchful eye of God; or Peter enjoying the hospitality of Simon the Tanner and gazing out over the foam-crested waves from the flat rooftop of his house.

Najji pulled our bus to the curb near the high point of the Old City, where we disembarked and began to look around. I had written a scene or two set in Jaffa when I was a teenager, penning an adventure story set amid the battles of the Third Crusade. I tried to imagine the city as it had looked with defensive battlements on every side and the armies of Europe encamped around it, and with my hero Martin looking up at the town with a curious and conflicted gaze.

But then something interrupted my reveries: a gull floated by above my head, and I knew it at a glance from my study—a Yellow-legged Gull. And then a White-spectacled Bulbul in a tree across the street. And then a pair of European Turtle-Doves and a Laughing Dove. I was racking up species for my list left and right, and had to tear myself away in order to join the rest of the group. They had gathered around Norah as she explained some of the history and notable sites of the ancient town.

As it happened, the place where we were standing was just a stone's throw from the traditional site of Simon the Tanner's house. It was easy to imagine Peter embracing his friend down at the end of the little alleyway; easier still to see him praying on the rooftop, where his vision of the unclean animals dropped down into view from the broad blue dome of the sky (Acts 10), just as the gull had dropped down for me a few moments earlier. There we were, level with the rooftops, in a city on a hill that overlooked the sea, and it felt as though the sky was all around us, and at any moment a celestial vision might break upon our gaze.

We paused there to have our first service of worship in the Holy Land. Our trip had been designed to include short segments of corporate song, prayer, and reflection at each of the sites along the way. And so everywhere we went,

we eleven wayfarers would pause to gather in a circle, sing a hymn, hear a recitation of a biblical story, and say a short prayer. Each of us had been assigned
a couple different New Testament stories to narrate during our pilgrimage.
I had also been thrust into an informal role as a worship leader; Josh would
often ask me to guide the singing. I was happy to do so when I could—our
guidebooks gave us traditional hymns to sing, sometimes with adapted lyrics,
and though I didn't know all of the selections, we were able to get through
most of the recommended ones. And so I found myself on a sun-washed street
atop Jaffa's ancient promontory, calling out the notes to "There's a Wideness in
God's Mercy." Josh led the service with a narration of Peter's vision.

There was something marvelous about this practice of doing devotions
together at every site. This was my first pilgrimage, so I have nothing to compare it against, but I've been told that many other pilgrimage tours make only
minimal efforts at including moments of reflection like these. I was grateful for
the intentionality of it: a reminder that we were there to experience the presence of Christ through the blessing of shared faith, prayer, and Scripture, and
not merely to parade like tourists through a bunch of dusty old towns. And
the way these services were designed—as participatory recitations of Bible
stories—brought an incarnational element to the experience. I wasn't simply
hearing the same stories I had heard a thousand times from the Gospels; I
was hearing them mediated through the voice, the heart, and the gifts of my
brothers and sisters in Christ. (Much of this intentional structure comes from
the work of Rev. Dr. Ken Parker, who had designed this style of pilgrimage
experience, and whom we had had the pleasure of meeting in our orientation
sessions back in Maine.)

But I also have to confess to a bit of spiritual greed—I wanted even more
than our little mini-services. All along the way, I was thirsting for more time, for
just a few more minutes to sit and pray in the places we visited—but that's just
not the way it goes on a trip like this. More time to pray means less chances to
visit once-in-a-lifetime places. Even beyond those rushed moments, though, I
had an even deeper longing, one that I hadn't even thought to propose during
the planning stages of the pilgrimage: I wanted to go to church in Israel. We
were coming to the Holy Land as pilgrims of the risen Lord; we would be in
Jerusalem on Sunday; but trips of this sort do not usually carve out time to
join with local congregations. I asked Norah if she thought it might be pos-

sible for me to head out on my own and find a church service in Jerusalem after our daily tour was done on Sunday, but she didn't think it wise.

I hadn't realized the depth of my desire until I was standing there in Israel, touring through churches and walking down streets where Israeli and Palestinian Christians lived. The profoundest, most deeply spiritual moments in all my many travels had come in churches, as I worshiped with brothers and sisters from different corners of the earth. We would see lots of sacred sites, but I did not want to miss out on the most sacred locus of all: the living, vibrant Body of Christ in those places. I longed for a chance to go to church in Israel, and I was feeling just a little heartsick to think that it wouldn't happen. Unfortunately, then, despite what I think were noble desires, I was not always able to invest myself in our group's mini-services as fully as I ought. But the fault is mine, and I suspect it reflects rather poorly on the breadth of my character. For who can say what richness of experience I missed by choosing to mourn an unlikely future rather than accepting the gift of the present moment?

———·———

We took a short walk around the summit of Jaffa's hill, bathed in the golden sunlight of late afternoon. From the road beside Simon the Tanner's house, we turned our steps up a lovely gardened walkway and through a lush park. Common Mynas and Hooded Crows strutted self-importantly here and there in the grass. There was a large colonial-style cathedral there, just a bit down the face of the bluff, its walls shining amber in the softness of the light. Set amid palm trees and flowering hedges, the church welcomed us to a place that was both exotic and, at the same time, the homeland of our hearts. We walked until we came to an overlook; and there, framed by a stone gateway, was a view of the gleaming towers of Tel Aviv, commanding the low plains just north of Jaffa. I took a few moments to pause in wonder: I knew enough of Tel Aviv's story to be duly impressed by its aspect, having sprung from the barrenness of dusty dunes to become this glimmering emblem of productivity.

We descended from the overlook park, down the edge of the bluff toward the church, and then into the high-walled alleys that made up the streets of Old Jaffa. These enclosed pathways were narrow and deep, like the passages of a great sandstone castle. Here and there were little artists' shops and wrought-iron balconies bedecked with flowers, but for the most part the streets were lined with unbroken brown walls. And every now and then, we came across doors that caught my attention—metal doors, painted in jet-black or brightest blue, with a square white cross set in the center. Above the cross were the letters "IC XC," and below it, "NIKA." This was an inscription I knew from my lovestruck study of ancient Christian tradition: the abbreviation of Jesus' name and the ascription of his great victory: "Jesus Christ conquers!" These were the doorways to an Orthodox monastery, built into the walls of Old Jaffa. And I, who had often longed for the life of a monk, paused and smiled.

OUR OWN NATIVE HOME

I cannot rest from travel: I will drink
Life to the lees....
For always roaming with a hungry heart
Much have I seen and known ...
I am a part of all that I have met;
Yet all experience is an arch wherethro'
Gleams that untraveled world whose margin fades
For ever and forever when I move....

—Alfred, Lord Tennyson, "Ulysses"

Eventually we emerged from the narrow streets of Old Jaffa and stepped out onto the edge of the harbor. There was a small quay with a few boats tied up, and then the sweeping scope of the blue Mediterranean. After a short walk along the broad harbor road, we reunited with Najji and his silver bus. We were tired and jet-lagged, but there was one more site in the area that Norah wanted to show us. Many of us probably would have declined if we were given the option, but she made the decision for us, and in the end we were glad she did. After a short drive over to Tel Aviv, we pulled up in a residential neighborhood next to a house that looked nothing like the brick-and-cement Middle Eastern homes all around. It was a wooden house with brown clapboard siding and a peaked roof, an exotic splash of New England in Israel.

We got out and looked around while Norah gave us the background on the place. It was called the Maine Friendship House, and it was the last remnant of an attempted settlement by a group of Mainers a century and a half before. In the late 1860s a shipload of people from Jonesport—a little seaside town in Downeast Maine, not far from my home—embarked on an adventure to settle in the Holy Land and to help encourage Jewish immigration there. The history of the settlement was a sad one; they were unprepared for what faced them, and most were reduced to poverty before being forced to leave. But the attempt itself, and what it represented, had remained a treasured part of modern Israeli history. Norah was excited to have a tour group from Maine so that she could share this connection that our state—unbeknownst to us— had had on the development of Israel.

We paused for a few moments to take pictures of the house in its restored setting, with a lovely steepled church standing alongside. It was one of the last things we had expected to find: a little chunk of Maine here in the Holy Land. But its presence, much as the warm familiarity of churches on every side, reminded us that this strange and distant land was, in a very real sense, our own native home.

———·———

The day ended with slow, weary grace as we piled back into Najji's bus and drove away from Tel Aviv. The sun was setting, and though our biological clocks were still under the impression that it was midday, many were yawning from the strain of poor sleep the night before. We drove north along the coast in the fading light, up toward the city of Netanya. There we came to the first of several marvelous hotels that would host us for our stay, set on the corner of a downtown plaza. Josh and I roomed together, and after a lovely meal, we retired to our beds.

I had already set plans to do something that my fellow pilgrims thought bordered on odd, if not outright mad: to thumb my nose at the cruel biolgical reality of jet lag, and rise one or two hours early every day to go out and look for birds. I had been assured by Norah and Scott that, with the exception of our stay in Jerusalem, it would be safe enough to wander out on my own in the early dawn. So that's what I did.

In the stillness of the day's awakening, I walked out of the hotel and onto the city street. I'm not much of a city person, as I've said before, but there is something magical about a city in the first light of dawn. The streets are quiet, still at rest, but there's a distinct excitement about them, a sense of anticipation and preparation. A few early risers are walking or driving through the empty streets. Shopkeepers are opening the locks and gates on their storefronts. Bakers are already sending haunting aromas wafting into the air. And all around, the stark gray concrete is cast in soft tones of coral and flame. For just a moment, in the crispness of the morning breeze, the ugliness of modern pavement and functional architecture shines like a jewel in the rays of the rising sun.

I slipped through Netanya's plaza and over to the bluffs that looked out to the sea. There was a little garden area there, planted with palm trees and flowers, and a walking path that curved around the top of the bluffs. And there, below, were the sandy beaches of the Mediterranean, against a western horizon that was just beginning to pick up a bit of rosiness from the eastern sky. I found a broad set of stairs that led down to the beach, and though all was still quiet and calm, there were a few other walkers about—mostly old men with calm, genial faces.

Already I began to spot the birds I sought. There were the usual suspects all about—after less than a day, I could recognize Hooded Crows, Common Mynas, and the widespread dove species at a single glance. But there were new ones, too—a Eurasian Blackcap and a Common Whitethroat, two Old World warblers, feeding in the bushes beside a stairway. And above my head wheeled dozens of swifts, cutting through the morning air with graceful, scythe-like sweeps.

I trudged along the beach for a while, watching the rising dawn behind the city on the bluff. I realized as I walked there that this might be my only chance to step into the waters of the Mediterranean Sea. So I slipped off my shoes, rolled up the bottoms of my jeans, and stepped into the waves. They were warm, but not as warm as I expected. There was still a bit of a chill in those April waters. Compared to dipping one's feet in the waves of Maine's coast, though, it was a paradise of comfort. I paused there for a long moment, thinking of the many scenes that had played out upon those waves, and then slowly made my way back up the stairs and across the plaza.

Later that day, we would be driving up into the hills to the place where it all began: the village of Nazareth, there to walk the paths of the Savior.

Part 2

"Tell Me the Story of Jesus"

Walking Through the Gospels

THE PLACE WHERE
IT ALL BEGAN

O Word of God incarnate, O Wisdom from on high,
O Truth unchanged, unchanging, O Light of our dark sky,
We praise Thee for the radiance that from the hallowed page,
A lantern to our footsteps, shines on from age to age.

—William How, "O Word of God Incarnate"

Our pilgrimage took us to many of the places mentioned in the Gospels, the sites of Jesus' life and ministry. We didn't visit them in any particular order save what efficiency and geography dictated. For the purposes of this book, I've chosen to arrange the remainder of the narrative according to the chronological account of the Gospels. That is, we will walk the paths of Christ as he walked them. The story begins, then, in Nazareth, with the angel's pronouncement to Mary that she would have a son.

Nazareth is set in the central hills of Galilee, after the ascent from the Mediterranean coast and before descending the other side, toward the Sea of Galilee. We approached the town from the west, driving up past the southern roots of the ridge of Mount Carmel. As trees and fields rolled by, I caught the bright, cotton-candy-blue flash of a bird, a European Roller, weaving its flight around the edge of the woods.

We could see Nazareth, or at least a part of it, as we drew near its hilltop aerie. It was now a rather large city and a center of Palestinian culture, and it spilled over the crest of the hills in a jumble of cement buildings. It was not, by any stretch of the imagination, what the Nazareth of Jesus' day would have looked like. But I knew that it would be like that, so I wasn't disappointed. It was enough of a thrill to simply be there, on those hilly slopes where my Lord grew up. Though the houses looked different, and there were far more of them now, the shape of the mountains would have been the same as those he saw, the blue overhead the same that he looked at every day, and (most importantly) the birds winging about were the same species he would have spied as a child, the same sparrows and doves that he referenced in his teaching.

We parked and walked the rising streets up to the vast, white-stone Basilica of the Annunciation, the great cathedral on the slope of the hill. This sprawling new church had been built atop the ruins of an older church, which had been built atop an even older one, and so on back to the early days of Byzantine Christian faith. The church was named, of course, after the story of the angel Gabriel appearing to Mary and proclaiming the incarnation of our Lord in Mary's womb. In short, this was the place where the eternal, infinite God took on our humble nature in the humblest of forms. There's good historical cause for believing this attribution; indeed, one of my guidebooks noted that the church and its grounds are so large that the basilica's footprint likely covers much of the first-century village of Nazareth, which probably amounted to only a few hundred people in a small cluster of homes.

Mary herself may or may not have been from Nazareth; the Gospels don't say one way or the other. But there is a very ancient Christian tradition which holds that she spent much of her early life in Jerusalem, very near the Temple precincts, and that it was only after her betrothal to Joseph that she moved up to Galilee. In fact, we visited the traditional birthplace of Mary in Jerusalem on our tour, a lovely spot marked by the Crusader church of Saint Anne (according to tradition, Mary's mother).

In a second-century document called the Protoevangelium of James, widely read in the early church, we're told that Mary, as a young virgin, had been selected as a weaver to help fashion a new veil for the Temple, the great curtain which hung before the Holy of Holies. This is not an implausible connection, since the story is set at the same time that King Herod was undertaking a massive renovation of the Temple precincts. In some paintings of the annunciation, Mary is portrayed at a loom or spinning wheel, in reference to this story. The Temple curtain represented the intersection of divine and human spaces in the Temple, where the area marked for the presence of God met the area marked for the priests' daily work. In that sense, it is a fitting symbol for Jesus Christ: the place where God and humanity, the divine nature and the human, intersect. Indeed, the author of Hebrews directly equates this curtain with Jesus' body (Heb. 10:20). We can't know for sure if the old story about Mary weaving the curtain is true; there's just not enough historical evidence to make a judgment with any confidence. But if it is, then it does add an interesting layer of symbolism to the Gospel accounts: Mary wove the curtain on her loom; the Son of God became flesh within her womb; and when Christ's body died on the cross, that very same curtain was torn in two (Matt. 27:51).

In any case, the Gospel of Luke introduces us to Mary when she's already in Nazareth, betrothed to Joseph and awaiting the beginning of their married life together. And then the angel Gabriel appears, commencing the most remarkable conversation in the history of the world. Gabriel tells Mary that she will conceive a son, and that he will be the Son of God and the long-awaited Messianic king. After asking how God intended to do such a thing, Gabriel replies that it will be done solely by the power of the Holy Spirit. At that, Mary immediately assents to God's plan: "I am the Lord's servant. May your word to me be fulfilled" (Luke 1:38).

Mary's reaction here is astounding. Though she no doubt realized what a great honor it was to bear the hope of Israel, she also surely would have known what a devastating position this put her in. She was as yet unmarried, and if she became pregnant, Joseph would likely break off their engagement (Matt. 1:18–19). Then she would be a pariah, cut off from her society because of its assumptions about her infidelity. She would be marked with shame, unlikely to find another marriage; and without a husband in that culture, she would have a very difficult time providing for herself and her son. Of course, as we know, Joseph did choose to marry her; but at that particular moment, Mary would only have known what the likeliest social outcomes were for her, and they looked bleak indeed. And yet, with the most gracious, humble submission to God's will, she immediately said yes.

This speaks volumes about Mary's character. Think of all the many heroes of the Old Testament who hesitated to accept God's calling, who tried their best to get out of it—Moses (Exod. 4:13), Barak (Judg. 4:4–9), Gideon (Judg. 6:15–17), Saul (1 Sam. 10:20–22), Jeremiah (Jer. 1:4–6), Jonah (Jon. 1:1–3), and more besides. Yet Mary gives an immediate, courageous "Yes" to God. Here at the beginning of the New Creation, as God sets in motion our restoration from the Fall, Mary does what Eve did not do: she obeys. And with her obedience, empowered by the proclamation of the gospel of Christ's coming, the long, thickly woven cord of human rebellion against God begins to unravel, and the Son of God, the Logos, enters his own creation so that his grace might be woven upon the loom of our hearts.

We gathered in a shaded colonnade to one side of the church's courtyard, beside a long display of artwork from many different nations, all portraying the wonder of the annunciation in their own respective styles and forms. It was there that I first served a turn as the group's narrator for one of our mini-services, reciting the story of Mary's interaction with Gabriel. It had been my first choice among the possible stories to narrate, partly because of my deep appreciation for the theology of the incarnation, which I had gained at the feet of the early church fathers, and partly because Mary and her story had become profoundly special to me personally. And to be right there, in that very place, speaking the story of her great, faithward affirmation of God's daring and costly plan for her life, and of the climactic moment when God revolutionized the fate of the whole human race—it nearly moved me to tears. In a voice made hoarse with emotion, I finished the story and led our group in song, and then we made our way into the vast, fascinating edifice of the church.

I CRIED OUT, AND
HE ANSWERED ME

It is no shame to have wept in Palestine.

—William C. Prime, *Tent Life in the Holy Land*

The church was split into two levels on the inside; both were broad, open spaces that connected with each other beneath the great rotunda of the dome. We went first into the lower level, which preserved elements of the ancient churches that had previously stood on the spot. (I'll have more to say about this lower level when we come to the story of Jesus' years of growing up in Nazareth.) Then having completed the downstairs circuit, we went to the upper section. It was toweringly vast, with soaring wooden beams that pulled one's gaze toward heaven. Far ahead, beneath a massive mural that formed the altarpiece, a small group of pilgrims was holding Mass together. In hushed whispers we followed our guide and took in some of the artwork around the sides of the nave. After this, we had the opportunity for what I truly wanted: just a few moments to rest silently in the peace of that place, and to pray.

I paused, closed my eyes, and thought about the story of the annunciation. In that moment, the power of Mary's "yes" was manifest to me by a stark contrast with my own experience. I too, and every Christian, had this call in our lives: that Christ may be formed in us (Gal. 4:19), though of course in a different sense than Mary's high calling. But while Mary simply said yes to God and then obediently followed, I felt that I jolted through life in fits and starts: part of my heart crying out a constant, desperate "yes!" to God while another part kept dragging me back. Every attempt at an all-encompassing life of disciplined, faithful obedience seemed to founder on the rocky reefs of my stubborn sinfulness. How I longed to live a life wholly devoted to God! I yearned to be like those heroic old desert monks, devoting every waking hour to prayer and the pursuit of holy obedience, battling upward as the good work of the Holy Spirit proceeded in their hearts, without the encumbrances of petty sins and self-centered living. I longed for victory—no, strike that: victory was too ambitious a goal for me; I simply longed for consistent progress in my great goal of living into the holiness with which God had clothed me through the grace of Jesus Christ. My desire was so deep and so palpable, my great yearning to live a saintly life, that it began to pour in tears down my cheeks as I sat in the great church of Nazareth. "God, give me just a small portion of Mary's valiant obedience," I prayed. "Help me to say a consistent yes to you, just as she did."

It was a prayer full of desolation and heartbreak—so much so that I was a little embarrassed that my feelings struck so deep. But amid that desolation, it was not a sad prayer. There was a peace about the experience, a richness that I can't quite describe. I felt the sort of exhausted relief a person might feel upon finally unburding their deepest longing to a trusted friend. After a time that seemed altogether too short, we ended our prayerful silence and walked over to the side of the church, where an exit from the upper level led us over some excavations of the first-century village.

It was then that something astounding happened, something which, as soon I saw it, struck me as having been intended entirely for me, in direct answer to my great, yearning heart-cry of a moment before. A single blackbird hopped out of the shadows and paused in the sunlight, cocking its head to look at us.

Now, I need to back up a little and explain why this was meaningful to me. I'm sure the reader will think it an insignificant event—"So, you walked out of the church and saw a bird!"—and in truth, I'm sure my fellow pilgrims didn't give that bird a second thought, if they noticed it at all. But it had a profound meaning for me. Here's why: as odd as it sounds, I have received a handful of interactions with birds that seemed to be intended as direct and poignant answers to my prayers or to the unspoken longings of my spiritual life. And it's important to say that when this happens (and it's very rare for me), it is almost always at a tremendously crucial juncture of my life; it is not at all the case that I am everywhere seeing birds and wishfully interpreting them as omens. Rather, it is simply that every once in a great while, God chooses to speak to his people in "sign language" (to borrow a phrase from one of my parishioners).

Let me give you another example, entirely true, if only to illustrate what I mean by all of this. One of the most profound such events was my first sighting of an American Kestrel, a bird that I had known as a boy only through pictures in field guides, but which I had adopted as my favorite animal and projected upon it an entire ethos of courageous living. When I played made-up super-heroes in my childhood, I was "the Kestrel"—and yet I had never actually seen one. My first sighting of a kestrel came on the rocky top of a small moun-tain years later, when I was a young man, as I opened my eyes to the heavens after praying that God would send me a sign. You see, I was feeling the quiet promptings of the Holy Spirit, pressing me to go over and talk to a group of fellow hikers. I had spent the previous weeks praying for opportunities to wit-ness and share the Gospel; but now here was an opportunity, and I wasn't sure I had the courage to take it. So I prayed for a sign, a confirmation that that was what God wanted me to do. Then I opened my eyes, and there was the kestrel, circling through the sky (no doubt commencing its fall migration southward)—the first kestrel I had ever seen: my icon of courageous living. It was the very kick in the pants I had asked for. So I went and witnessed to those people, and had a long and friendly conversation with them about faith and the love of God.

This pattern held true for my relationship with Eurasian Blackbirds. I had never seen one before that moment in Nazareth—they're an Old World spe-cies, so I had no occasion to see them in Maine. Nevertheless, I knew about them and had come to adopt them as a particular symbol in the spiritual life.

A few years previously, I had come across a story from the life of a Celtic saint, Kevin of Glendalough. The legend says that on Ash Wednesday he was praying out on a hillside above his monastery, his arms stretched out cruciform-style to the heavens. While he was praying, a blackbird came and landed on his hand. He didn't move, for fear of startling the bird—he just kept praying. The blackbird then flew away and returned with straw in its beak. And little by little, it built a nest in Saint Kevin's outstretched hand. So Kevin just kept praying. By a miracle of endurance, he stood there and prayed while the blackbird laid eggs, sat on them, hatched them, fed its young, and then fledged them out of the nest. The legend says that from Ash Wednesday to Easter, he prayed unmoving on that hillside.

This little tale struck me powerfully. Not only did it connect with my love for birds, but it was a beautiful symbol of persevering in prayer. I even wrote a poem about it at the time (which you can read in the appendix). All that to say, for several years prior to my Israel trip, blackbirds had come to symbolize a life of patient, prayerful obedience to the call of God, humbly persevering even through long trials and silences.

And now, having just walked out of the church of Nazareth, where I had poured out my heart regarding my failures to live a life of consistent holiness—at that precise moment, I saw my first blackbird. It felt as if God had taken me by the shoulders and looked straight into my eyes to say, "Keep going. I hear your prayers. I know your longing. Like Saint Kevin, keep going. Seek me in the perseverance of prayer, and don't give up. I know your heart, and I am with you on this journey."

It is hard to express just how profoundly sweet that moment was. There, in Nazareth itself, I cried out to God, asking him to help me, like Mary, say my "Yes!" to him, and he had responded by pouring out a "Yes!" to me—not just a yes to my prayer request, but a "Yes!" to my whole being, to the whole scope of the journey which I walked. God saw my longing for holiness, and said yes, and he saw me toiling in the midst of my sins and failings, and he said yes to that too. And perhaps that's the great truth of the annunciation after all—that it wasn't just about Mary's "yes" to God, but much more that in this moment and in this act of incarnation, God was saying a triumphant, eternal "Yes!" to the whole human experience. One of my favorite titles for Christ in Scripture has always been the way he describes himself in Revelation 3:14, as "the Amen"—God's great, loving "Yes!" to all of us.

MY BETHLEHEM BACKSTORY

Oh make this heart rejoice or ache;
Decide this doubt for me;
And if it be not broken, break—
And heal it, if it be.

—William Cowper, "The Contrite Heart"

We were now on our way to Bethlehem, to see and bear witness at the site of Jesus' birth. But we also visited, just briefly, another stop nearby: the hill-palace of King Herod, Herodium. Most of our stops along the tour were in-depth, substantial, and deeply connected to the story of the Gospels. But Herodium was not. It was a pause, made in passing, to take a brief glance at a world which had been set in opposition to Bethlehem, but a world which has since been forgotten. You see, for two millennia now it has been Bethlehem's towering legacy which defined the meaning of those places—it is, after all, the spot where the Son of God was born. But at the time of that event, as the years turned from what we now call BC to AD, it was Herodium, not Bethlehem, that drew everyone's gaze.

Herod, known to Christians as the villain in the early pages of the Gospels, was known in the ancient world as Herod the Great. And when one visits Israel, even two thousand years later, it's not hard to see why. He was known far and wide for his monumental construction projects, feats of engineering which still boggle the mind today. At Masada, at Herodium, at the Temple Mount, and at Caesarea Maritima, his works testify to the ambitious genius of this builder-king. He may have been cruel, immoral, and despotic, but he and his men could build wonders; and though he was just a puppet-king under Rome, he was renowned throughout the Empire. Herodium was one of those works, a hilltop palace complex where, according to tradition, he was laid to rest at the end of his life. So if Bethlehem is the city of faith, Herodium is the palace of the world, set in opposition to God, but clothing its lust for power in wonders of art, engineering, and creativity as audacious as the Tower of Babel had been.

We didn't stay long at Herodium; didn't even go up to look at the ruins. We just stood at the curb on the side of the hill, looking out over the fields of Tekoa, where the prophet Amos once lived. A Hoopoe flew by below us on the hillside, and swooped down to probe among the rocks until it came up with a beetle. Hoopoes, with their pastel orange plumage, funky crests, curving beaks, and zebra-stripe wings, are among the strangest-looking birds in the world. They're one of the species of birds mentioned in the Bible, but they're noted there only because they're counted as unclean (Lev. 11:13–18). It was a delightful sighting, but it also seemed to match the spiritual narrative of the place. The hoopoe is a strange, but strangely charismatic bird, and it was fitting to see it there, at our brief stop at the alternative world that Herod had tried so hard to create. Because, you see, I had also made a brief stop in the story of my life some years before, to pause and consider the question of whether Herodium might be telling a truer story than Bethlehem did.

Bethlehem is an essential stop on any Christian pilgrimage, as it had been since the days of the early church. The story of Christmas is so intimately interwoven with our faith as to make it difficult to imagine the Gospel without Christmas. But I did, once, imagine it so. And my faith nearly fell apart. Part of the story of my season of doubt is a story about Bethlehem, and about turning away from it, just for a moment, to a world apart from God.

I was already a long ways into my "dark night of the soul" (as described in the Part 1 chapter "Leaving Home"), wrestling with why God would have abandoned me, why he would have stripped my soul of all the spiritual consolations that had kept me connected to him for so long. It was early in the season of Advent, with our home all decked out for Christmas. And as I sat down to study Christ's birth narratives in Matthew and Luke, I suddenly realized that I had to at least consider the possibility that my faith—my whole life of faith—had been in error. In order to be intellectually honest, I had to do what Socrates had advised of old: follow the argument wherever it goes. And the birth narratives are one of those places where the argument, on both sides, is easy to see.

Matthew and Luke tell different stories about the birth of Christ—not contradictory stories, to be clear, but different stories. Whereas much of the material of their Gospels is held in common, they use entirely different material in the birth narratives. Why is this so? Christians have always said that the two narratives are complementary—far from contradicting each other, each narrative picks authentic stories which fit with the theological goals of the text. When the two texts are held together, you get the complete story of Christmas which is so familiar to us all. Besides, the use of different but complementary stories might easily be explained if Matthew or Luke had knowledge of the other's work, and there's some evidence that one or the other may have.

But to skeptics, the birth narratives show a very different picture. It's easy to make a case that the stories are different because both authors, independently, knew they needed to explain why the prophesied Messiah from Bethlehem had actually come from Nazareth instead, and so each fabricated a story. Unfortunately, like suspects being grilled by investigators in separate rooms, they each made up a different version of the story.

I had known both sides of this argument for a long time, but for some reason, in my disillusioned spiritual state, the skeptical argument hit me with tremendous force just then. What if it really was all just made up, a lie invented to cover an inconvenient mismatch between Jesus' actual birthplace and where the biblical prophecies clearly said he should have been born? And if the story of Christmas were untrue, what reason did I have for believing the interwoven accounts about the virgin birth? And if not the virgin birth, then how could I believe in the incarnation of the Son of God? And if not the incarnation, then Jesus of Nazareth was just another man, and my faith was senseless, and the world I had known my whole life was desperately hollow. I fell to my knees and wept.

It felt like a tipping-point, the moment I knew I had to turn and follow the evidence with whatever courage I could muster, and see where it led. It's worth saying that this was not a rebellion, not a willful turning away from God to pursue my own agenda for life as an independent spirit. Rather, it was a heartbroken, devastating loss, and I was disconsolate to think that I may have only myself, and no longer have God. But I wanted to have the truth; I needed to have the truth; and not even my own heartbreak would sway me from that quest.

I spent a while thinking of myself as an agnostic Christian (a strange term, I know, but it was the best I could come up with at the time)—culturally, aesthetically, and morally bound to this religion that I loved—but open to skepticism about its doctrine. I read a lot of tremendously good, hard books; learned more about physics and philosophy than I had ever known before; and had many long dialogues in which I tested the saintly patience of my brother, Josh, by constantly playing the devil's advocate. The truth was, despite all my prayer and all my research, I felt like there were compelling strands tugging me in both directions simultaneously. Sometimes, physics and philosophy would pull me back and remind me that I couldn't renounce the God who had absented himself from me; at other times, the art, the culture, and the pervasive metanarrative of our secular world became so eloquent that Herodium made more sense than Bethlehem. In the end, I felt caught in the middle.

And then a miracle happened—if you can believe it, a Christmas miracle. God gave me back my faith. It's difficult to explain it any better than that. Rational arguments—enormously compelling ones—would follow, buttressing my new understanding; but it all began with what happened to me on another Advent morning, almost exactly two years since I had fallen down and wept at the crumbling façade of the Christmas story.

Some parts of this story I will leave untold, but I think I can describe enough of it so the reader gets a sense of just what a transformative moment it was. It was a bright December morning, with a blanket of snow on the ground outside, and I was doing some reading. I knelt down on the floor to retrieve a book from a low shelf, and by a vague impulse of idle curiosity, I grabbed a different book—a volume of early-church theology written by an Orthodox priest—and flipped it open. I can't remember today what the exact words were that I read, but I remember the result: all of the sudden an enormous, overwhelming consciousness of the presence of God swept over me like a tidal wave. Something indescribable, something numinous had blown through my soul with all the warmth and wildness of a tropical hurricane, and I knew—I knew!—the reality of God as I had never known it before.

It felt as if I had been a blind man, and my vision was restored to me for the very first time. And I mean that literally: I could *see* the world in a different way than I had ever seen it before. It wasn't a seeing with my physical eyes, but with a perception of the soul I had never been granted before. I looked at my surroundings and I saw from the innermost depths of my being, that everything around me was alive with the presence of God. To be clear, this wasn't pantheism, or anything like it: rather, it was as if the veil had been pulled back for just a moment, so that I could see things as they really were, as described by the angels' cry in Isaiah 6: "The whole earth is full of his glory." This sensation lasted for several minutes. The world around me was suffused with the holiness of God's presence, very much as in Elizabeth Barrett Browning's poem: "Earth's crammed with heaven, and every common bush afire with God."

Over the next few days, I devoured every book of early-church theology I could find. And in the process, God rewove the Christmas story into my heart and mind. I discovered the consistency and beauty of the ancient Christian traditions about the birth narratives: there never was any other alternate story, simply this compelling, beautiful tale of the miracle of Bethlehem, reinforced by historical memories that were recorded in other early Christian texts.

So, in this vastly roundabout way, I had come back to the Christmas story, and now it was far more personal and precious to me than it had ever been before. Whereas I had once felt almost a stranger to my own faith, now it was like home again. So as our bus rolled up the roads to Bethlehem, it felt like a homecoming, for the story of Christmas had become the story of my soul.

THE CITY OF THE LOWLY

Come to your heaven, you heavenly choirs!—
Earth hath the heaven of your desires.
Remove your dwelling to your God:
A stall is now his best abode.

—Robert Southwell, "New Heaven, New War"

Before we entered the center of Bethlehem, we paused at a place that had once been well outside the village but was swallowed up by the spreading city. This was the location known as Shepherds' Field, one of the possible sites where the shepherds from Luke's account had received their angelic visitation announcing the birth of Christ.

Though much of the landscape around the site had been altered by the changes of time, a thin strip of wild grassland remained, dotted with a few trees. At the far end of this narrow field was a church commemorating the event. It was small but lovely, made to be a way station for praying pilgrims, not a parish church. A little altar stood in the middle, around which ran a pillared passage with benches and artwork. But the real wonder of the church was in its lighting. Beams of light cascaded from the dome overhead, piercing through hundreds of miniscule openings meant to resemble the stars of the night sky. And around the dome were images of angels, along with the Latin translation of their great doxology: "Glory to God in the highest, and on earth peace to those on whom his favor rests!"

Our leader, Scott, encouraged us to sing Christmas carols there, so as we walked along the outer arcade I began to sing "O Come, All Ye Faithful." The rest of our group joined in, and the little church was transformed into an echo chamber of song. Even lovelier still, other pilgrims heard the song and joined in, each in their own language. One of them was singing in Latin, the hymn's original tongue. When that was done, we chorused through other carols too, like "Angels We Have Heard on High" and "Hark! The Herald Angels Sing."

A lovely fountain just beside the church depicts one of the shepherds. I've always appreciated the story of the shepherds, because it reveals God's intentional, outreaching concern for even the poorest and most overlooked of people. Shepherds in Jesus' day were often considered rustics, and untrustworthy ones at that, suspected of using land that was not their own to graze their flocks by night. More than that, they were often forced by the necessities of their work and its seasonal schedule to live much of their life in a state of ceremonial uncleanness, meaning that shepherds were not always able to perform the required acts of worship in the Temple. Though there was still romance attached to the idea of shepherding—the great King David had been a shepherd, after all—it was the idealized version more than the reality that carried appeal. Shepherds were often shunned and neglected. Shepherding was lowly work, even in David's day; that's why he, the smallest and youngest of the brothers, had that as his task. And yet it was to these ones—the lowliest ones—that God chose to announce his glorious message of grace. The coming of the Son of God was an event that merited a triumphal parade through the streets of the capital, and a reception by the king at the palace and by the high priest at the Temple. Instead, the Son of God came humbly and quietly, to the lowliest of all.

There was a little cave-chapel just below and behind the church, a remnant of the place where the shepherds were said to have rested while their flocks grazed around them. I don't think it's just by chance that shepherds were chosen, nor that Christ was born in a stable. One of the inescapable features of the Christmas story, especially in Luke's gospel, is the presence of animals. The shepherds in their fields, the stable, and the manger form a refrain, and remind us, repeatedly, of the animals that were there. It's almost impossible to find a painting of the nativity that doesn't have a sheep, a donkey, a cow, or a camel somewhere in it.

It seems appropriate to have animals in the scene. In early Christian theology, one of the central points of understanding was that God, through his Son Jesus, had begun the process of the New Creation. This is made clear in much of the writings of the early-church fathers, and you can find open hints of it in the New Testament, as for instance, in 2 Cor. 5:17. Jesus was taken to be the new Adam, and through his death and resurrection to have forged a new humanity, of which we can become a part through faith in him (Rom. 5:12–19; 1 Cor. 15:22, 45). Further, this work of restoration in Christ will not ultimately be limited to humanity, but will one day encompass all of creation (Rom. 8:19–22). As such, just as Adam's story begins with being formed and placed in the Garden of Eden, surrounded by animals, isn't it fitting that the new Adam, the architect of the New Creation, begins his story surrounded by animals as well? It's a stirring foreshadowing of the great restoration for all creation that will one day come through Christ.

IN THE MIDDLE OF A MIRACLE

The stall where he cried as a baby can be best honored in silence; for words are inadequate to speak its praise… Behold, in this poor crevice of the earth the Creator of the heavens was born!

—Jerome, *Letter 46*

M y visit to the Church of the Nativity was one of the most powerful moments of my life. At first, however, it looked like it might be shaping up as nothing more than an onerous experience of touristy madness.

I was excited to see this church—other than the Church of the Holy Sepulchre in Jerusalem, nothing was higher on my list of sites. I had done some research on it before we came, and so I knew that the massive, blockish building in front of me was the oldest church building we would visit in Israel, and that it had one of the most spectacular histories attached to it. Portions of the existing structure of the fortress-like white church dated to the days of Constantine and his mother, Helena, in the fourth century, and it still bore prominent reminders of the work of Emperor Justinian and, later, the Crusader kings, who renovated and beautified the sanctuary.

One of the odd things about the church, though, is that to enter it, one has to stoop down low in order to get through a tiny, narrow doorway which serves as the only official entrance. The logic behind the doorways construction—which would never satisfy today's fire codes—was determined by the depredations the church had suffered during waves of raiders and invaders. The guardians of the church had found it better to have a door that a hostile horseman couldn't ride straight through. Although the reason for the door's shortness is practical, there's a fittingness to it, too. It's known as the Door of Humility, and it seems exactly right that to enter the place where the eternal God humbled himself to enter our sorrow-struck existence, we poor mortals should be forced to bow our heads in reverence.

Inside, the church is a bewildering jumble of grandeur and dilapidation. The nave is vast—in fact, there are five parallel naves in the basilica, marked off by four sets of monumental pink-marble pillars. The remnants of gleaming, gold-plated mosaics shimmer from the walls of the clerestory above, and in certain sections the floors have been opened up to reveal the ancient tile designs of the Constantinian walkways underneath. Major parts of the church are being restored, so there is scaffolding and plastic sheeting here and there. At the front is a massive Greek Orthodox iconostasis, though tarnished with age, so it has lost a good deal of its attractiveness. And strung from wires are what appear to be gaudy Christmas-ball decorations—not a conventional choice in Orthodox decorating, but, considering the Christmas associations of the church, they made an odd sort of sense.

Most jarring of all was the vast line of pilgrims waiting for their chance to get down into the Grotto of the Nativity, a small crypt set below the altar. According to some plausible historical traditions, that grotto was the original cave that served as the stable where Jesus Christ was born, and the whole vast edifice of the church had later been built around it. It is, of course, a matter of historical conjecture as to whether this particular spot was the true site of Jesus' birth. As with most of these ancient sites, however, its pedigree goes back much further than any other rival spot, and the setting of its location is a good match for the Gospel accounts.

The line of pilgrims wound back and around and through the columned naves, Disneyland-style, amounting to hundreds upon hundreds of people. Because we were a very small tour group, the Palestinian guards were willing to make some concessions for us—instead of waiting in the winding line, we were asked to sit for a while before the great iconostasis, and then again for a while longer in one of the side-chapels. I spent the time drinking in the sights and sounds around me, looking at all the beautiful, age-worn icons on the walls. (Some months later, I was flipping through a book of nineteenth-century watercolors of Holy Land sites, and saw that those very same icons had been on the walls back then, too.)

Finally, we got the signal that we could join the line. But *line* is probably not the right word. It was more of a vast caravan of people—a long, sinuous processional at least ten people across that slowly inched its way toward the funnel-like stairs that led down into the grotto. We were packed in together with these other pilgrims from all around the world, bodies pressed up against bodies, shuffling our feet when every new space of a few inches opened up in front of us. When we got to the ancient semicircle of stairs that fed down into one tiny doorway at the bottom, I got the chance to look at the faces of the pilgrims around me.

And that's where the wonder started. Here were pilgrims who, like us, had endured long travels just to get to this spot, and then waited arduous hours for this very moment. Now, as we were so near to it, we were being jammed together like sardines, uncomfortably sharing the same space and the same air. It would have been a perfect recipe for bitter, disgruntled attitudes and weary self-centeredness. But that's not what I saw. The faces looking back at me were weary, to be sure—but they were also alive with a sense of hope that is difficult to describe. They gazed down at that little doorway with a yearning that spoke more eloquently than any words.

Immediately I realized that I was witnessing a miracle. Norah had commented earlier in our pilgrimage that she loved seeing all the travelers from different countries, even if it made for the annoyance of busy lines and long waits. We were taking part in the fulfillment of the words spoken thousands of years ago by the prophets: that one day all nations would go up to Israel to worship the one true God. Here, on that stairway down to the Christmas stable, I was part of that millennia-long fulfillment. I, and all those around me, gathered from many different countries, were driven by the very same love.

We were brothers and sisters in Christ, and we were there because we all loved Jesus above all else.

The group that we were wedged in the middle of looked to be Orthodox Christians from Russia or eastern Europe. And as we all got to the bottom of the stairs and one by one squeezed through the stone-cut gap that made for a door, they broke out into song around me. I didn't recognize the tune; it was closer to a chant than any of our Western hymns are, but I knew it had to be a Christmas carol of some kind, a celebration of the birth of Christ. But whatever it was, the effect was sheer joy. Everyone was singing, some were crying, many were smiling immense, beaming smiles of wonder. And I, a stranger in a strange land, was suddenly in the midst of brothers, and we were all one family in the all-encompassing love of God.

Once again, as many times before in Israel, this felt exactly right: I, for whom the Christmas story had become so personally precious through my journey of doubt and renewal, and who had been helped back to my faith through the influence of Orthodox theologians, now stood in the very place the mystery happened, with Orthodox hymns ringing in my ears. When my turn came, I knelt down on the floor and reached in to touch the center of the fourteen-pointed star that marked the place where the Son of God was born. To be there, to touch the ground of the ancient stable, to smell the incense and hear the praises—it was a brief moment, but powerful.

From the very beginning, the stable where Jesus was born has drawn together the unlikeliest of pilgrims, the lowly and the proud, from the farthest reaches of the earth. Beginning with the humble shepherds and the wise men from the East, Bethlehem has summoned the nations to worship the God of Israel, and I was glad to be a part of that grand procession.

We took a few more moments to explore the grotto, looking at the little alcove where, by tradition, Jesus was laid in the manger. I strolled around the passageways to look at the art and touch the locked door that led to the chamber of Jerome, an early-church father. When finally it was time to go up and out, I saw the graffiti etchings of a thousand ancient crosses on the sides and lintel of the doorway—a final reminder that millions had passed this way before, over the course of centuries upon centuries and, like me, they had loved their Savior here.

WINGS OVER THE WALL

The angels keep their ancient places;—
Turn but a stone, and start a wing!
'Tis ye, tis your estrangèd faces,
That miss the many-splendored thing.

—Francis Thompson, "The Kingdom of God"

After his birth in Bethlehem, and when the time of purification was complete, Jesus was taken up to Jerusalem to be presented at the Temple. We visited the area of the Temple Mount on two different days of our tour, and I'll save some of those reflections for when we reach the story of Christ's passion. The part I'll tell here has to do with our time at the Western Wall, one of the most impressive remnants of the Temple complex that stood at the time of Jesus.

Najji dropped us off at one of the main gates in Jerusalem's outer wall, and from there we entered the city on foot. Tracing our way through the dim, canopy-covered market streets of Jerusalem, we worked our way back toward the Temple Mount. Much of the heart of Jerusalem is a web of market stalls lined around narrow lanes and shielded from the sun by a series of shades that span the gaps between buildings. All around us, a sea of humanity wove in and around each other—Christian clerics, Hasidic and Orthodox Jews, men in Muslim prayer caps, Israeli youths in combat fatigues, and lounging shopkeepers on every side. It certainly had the feel of a Middle Eastern bazaar, something I might have expected to find in nineteenth-century Cairo or Istanbul, and it was a winsome experience to see this side of Jerusalem, if only for a few minutes.

We emerged from the markets, and after passing through a security checkpoint, came out to the plaza beneath the Western Wall, that section of the Temple Mount's supporting wall that for centuries has played host to faithful Jews offering prayers and mourning the Temple's destruction (thus leading to its common name, the Wailing Wall). This section of wall has been standing since before Jesus' boyhood, and it is one of the last remnants of the Second Temple. Since this wall was the part of the supporting structure nearest to the Holy of Holies, rabbis have long taught that God's holy presence, the Shekinah, continued to dwell there at the wall, even after the Temple's destruction in AD 70.

The plaza by the wall is separated into distinct sections for men's and women's prayers, and so every member of our group had a designated area that we could approach to offer a prayer. It was not as busy as I expected, and there were many openings for us to go up and take a place at the wall. There were, as one might expect, many men there in traditional, Jewish Hasidic dress, but it was clear that there were also a fair number of Christians like us, drawn there out of reverence for what the Temple represented in the story of our faith. Indeed, by going to the Temple Mount to pray, we were reenacting the worship of the earliest Christians in Jerusalem, who still observed the regular prayer hours at the Temple courts. I laid a hand against the wall, feeling its rough surface and imagining all the devout men across the ages who had prayed there before me. I leaned my forehead against the wall and breathed out a prayer.

———·———

The presentation of Jesus in the Temple is remarked upon at great length in Luke's Gospel, and its remembrance became a major feast of the church calendar: the Feast of the Presentation (also called Candlemas). In my Baptist tradition, though, we scarcely ever throw a spare thought to this particular story. We tend to give all our attention during Advent to the birth narratives themselves, and then move on to other Scriptures and other studies. So the Presentation of the Lord, as a post-Christmas part of the story, sometimes gets overshadowed or forgotten.

But it's a momentous story, and worth our attention. It represents the coming of the Lord to his Temple—one of the greatest hopes of postexilic Israel, a day for which faithful Jews had yearned for hundreds of years. And to understand that hope, we need to back up in history a bit. The Temple—and the Tabernacle before it—were built as God-ordained places for his presence to dwell among his people. Within the inner sanctum, the Holy of Holies, the glorious presence of God himself—the Shekinah—was said to rest. The Temple was, in a sense, a representation of God's plan for the whole world. God designed the world with the intention of communing with his creation in the Garden of Eden, as in a "holy of holies" for the cosmos; and scholars both ancient and modern have remarked at how the layouts of the Tabernacle and Temple mirror the Creation accounts. This parallel between Temple and Creation is seen at its climax in the great scene of the new heavens and new earth in Rev. 21–22, where Temple language and Creation language are tightly interwoven to show that the consummation of all things is, indeed, all about God dwelling in our midst.

When the first Temple was built in Jerusalem—Solomon's Temple— its Holy of Holies housed the Ark of the Covenant, just as the Tabernacle had before it. This was the most sacred object in all of Israel, and for good reason: it was said to be the place where the Shekinah glory of God came to rest. In fact, the lid of the ark, called in Greek a *hilasterion* (sometimes translated "mercy seat") is referred to in Scripture in the manner of a throne. It was flanked by statues of cherubim (throne angels), and was conceived to be a direct reflection of the heavenly throne itself: "The Lord reigns; let the earth tremble; he sits enthroned between the cherubim" (Ps. 99:1). No wonder the Israelites treated the Holy of Holies and the Ark of the Covenant with such a weighty sense of awe, for there the King of the universe was enthroned in their midst.

After hundreds of years of spiritual rebellion by God's people, though, tragedy struck. God allowed the rising empire of Babylon to sweep through, decimate Jerusalem, and carry off its treasures and citizens into exile. Solomon's Temple was destroyed, and the Ark of the Covenant vanished from history. Many historians suspect it was destroyed in the Babylonian attack, or captured and melted down for its gold. Other ancient traditions hold that the prophet Jeremiah (or an angel) hid the Ark of the Covenant before the attack. But in either case, it was gone. Even after the Jews returned and rebuilt Jerusalem and the Temple, the Ark of the Covenant was no longer there. The Holy of Holies was vacant throughout the Second Temple period.

By Jesus' time, the Temple had been renovated by Herod's laborers into a truly spectacular work of architectural beauty, but there was still no Ark of the Covenant. Most Jews believed that the presence of God continued to dwell there, and went to worship at the Temple just as they were instructed to do in the Law. But there was a nagging sense throughout Jewish society that their exile hadn't ended at all. Many of them had returned home from Babylon, but they were still in a strange period of spiritual barrenness: no Ark of the Covenant, no prophets for four hundred years; and some sectors of Jewish society thought the established priesthood was corrupt and illegitimate.

Yet the great hope persisted that one day, perhaps, God would become manifest in his Temple again, as he did of old, and that he would reign, enthroned in the Holy of Holies, in the full splendor of his Shekinah glory. According to some ancient Jewish traditions, one of the expected outcomes of the Messiah's appearance was that he would restore the Ark of the Covenant to the Temple. That is, when the Messiah came, God would dwell and reign in their midst again. As the great messianic prophecy of Malachi foretold, "I will send my messenger, who will prepare the way before me. Then suddenly the Lord you are seeking will come to his temple; the messenger of the covenant, whom you desire, will come" (Mal. 3:1)

When Jesus comes to the Temple for the first time as a baby, it is a pivotal moment. Jesus represents the presence of God returning to the Temple courts. Simeon, upon seeing the baby Jesus there, speaks of "light" and "glory" in reference to Jesus, calling to mind the Shekinah glory of God. Later, when Jesus begins his ministry, he preaches a message that many of his followers would have connected to Temple terminology: he declares the reign of God (often translated as the kingdom of God), an idea associated with God's presence in the Holy of Holies, and suggests that this reign is now directly at hand, accessible (see, for example, Mark 1:15; Matt. 3:2, 13:31–32; Luke 17:21). The reign of God is now no longer localized to a single room in the Temple, but is out and about in the person of Jesus Christ, and will grow to fill the earth. And when Paul speaks about Jesus and what he did for us, he refers to Christ as a *hilasterion*—the word for the mercy-seat, the throne-cover of the ark that marked the spot where God's presence reigned in power (Rom. 3:25—in this passage, *hilasterion* is usually translated as "sacrifice of atonement" or "propitiation," because the mercy seat was where the highest rituals of atonement were completed). When the promised Messiah comes to the Temple—who himself is Immanuel, the presence of God dwelling among his people—it is the breathtaking summit of centuries of hope and expectation, and it sets the stage for the full grandeur of what Christ had come to do.

———·———

Standing at the Western Wall of the Temple Mount, I stepped back to take in my surroundings. I thought about how the immense, ineffable Shekinah glory of God had been hidden within the Temple all those ages ago, only revealed to the wondering eyes of the people on the rarest of occasions. And I thought of how his glory still, even now, is often seen, though unperceived by physical eyes, in the Body of Christ: in a building back then, in my brother and sister today, in the simple routine of gathering in the same pews, with the same people, every single week. Indeed, the Bible offers hints that God's glory, the weight of his unimaginable reality, is indeed all around us, pressing through everything we see and hear. "Where can I flee from your presence?" David asks in his psalm. "If I go up to the heavens, you are there. If I make my bed in the depths, you are there" (Ps. 139:7–8).

As I reflected on these things, I began to notice something wonderful in the sky overhead. Many dozens of swifts, perhaps as many as a hundred, were arcing in flight around and above the Western Wall. Like the birds of Psalm 84:3, they seemed to have made their nests in the wall of the ancient Temple, as if longing to be near the presence of God. These dark little birds, with wings that curve gently back like a scythe, alternate between rapid flutters and graceful, swooping glides that make them look like crescent moons cutting through the sky. I couldn't help but smile. I had seen other swifts in Israel, but never in concentrations like this.

But the main reason I smiled was this: swifts were one of the birds that I had sought for years. There's only one species of swift in my home area—the Chimney Swift—and though swifts weren't uncommon, for some reason I often drew blanks when I went looking for them. For the longest time, they weren't resident in my hometown, nor my parents' hometown, nor my in-laws' hometown. Finally, just the previous year, I had seen my first Chimney Swift swooping over the roofs of my town—but still just one, far from a common sighting. Every time I saw that lone swift, it felt like a special thrill. Now here I was, surrounded by the graceful, elegant dance of flocks of swifts wheeling in the air. The thing I had sought for so long, with so few results, now poured out like floodwaters. It seemed like the winsome hint of a promise: that perhaps someday my fervent yet fruitless desire to see the sweep of holiness' flight through the skies of my life might one day, suddenly, offer me the chance to look up and see a rush of wings.

My swift-story has another ending that occured some weeks after I left Jerusalem. That summer, back in my hometown, I gazed up with wonder to see that the once-vacant skies above our roofs were now filled with the swooping glides of more than a dozen swifts. The splendor of God's holy presence was not for the Temple alone, but for the streets of my everyday life. Now I see them over my house; I hear their gentle, chittering voices singing out as I walk; I see them above my church on Sundays. Every time I see them, I think of the Temple, and of the cry of the angels: "The whole earth is filled with his glory!"

A SHOOT FROM
THE STUMP OF JESSE

I pray, O Master, let me lie,
As on thy bench the favored wood;
Thy saw, thy plane, thy chisel ply,
And work me into something good.

—George MacDonald, "The Carpenter"

All of Jesus' boyhood years, aside from an early sojourn in
Egypt and periodic trips to Jerusalem, were spent in Nazareth, up in the hills of Galilee. There's a plausible historical argument (put forward by the archaeologist Bargil Pixner, among
others) that the town of Nazareth was intentionally settled by the
clans descended from Judah's royal line, of which Joseph was a
part. These clans, it is believed, maintained a strong family interest in their heritage and in the prophecies of a messiah who would

emerge from their midst, and they had several areas of settlement, including Bethlehem, the regions bordering the Sea of Galilee, and Nazareth itself. This may explain the fact that Nazareth appears to have been named with a messianic prophecy in mind: its name is derived from the Hebrew word *netzer*, referencing a new shoot that emerges at the base of an older stump, as in Isaiah's prophecy: "A shoot will come up from the stump of Jesse" (Is. 11:1).

If the town indeed had a strong local culture tied to family heritage and messianic expectations, it might explain some of the reactions of Jesus' neighbors and family to his ministry, as recorded in the Gospels—it is often the case that when expectations are strongly held and highly particular, then frustration, confusion, and disappointment are the natural result, which is the very thing we see from the Nazarenes during Jesus' ministry years. But whether or not the "royal clan" argument is true, it's marvelous to note just how fitting a thing it is for Jesus to have grown up in a town named Nazareth, for he was indeed the *netzer* coming forth from the stump of Jesse.

During our visit to Nazareth, we saw two sites that helped frame our understanding of what Jesus' boyhood life in the village might have been like. One of them is a ministry called Nazareth Village, which has purchased and preserved a small chunk of Nazareth in its more-or-less pristine, undeveloped state, and there re-created a first-century Jewish village. We arrived there close to midday, and sat down to share an authentic Middle Eastern meal, complete with the sorts of foods that Jesus would have been familiar with: bread and lentils, olives and figs, and hummus. Though it may have been a stretch for the American palates of a few in our group, I loved it: it brought me right back to my days of missionary service in North Africa, to bright times in my early twenties, scooping warm bread through *fuul* bean soup on a sun-washed street corner. It struck me that this was exactly the sort of meal portrayed in the Gospels, and I don't just mean the type of foods consumed. Eating with Jesus is always portrayed as a large-group activity, full of rich conversation and good companionship. Though I appreciated much of what was yet to come in my tour of Nazareth Village, that shared table of lentil soup was perhaps the moment that made me feel closest to the experience of Jesus' life as it had been in his old hometown.

After our lunch, we went on a tour of the historical reconstruction at Nazareth Village. There were period-costume actors dressed for the roles of carpenter, stoneworker, shepherd, and so on. There was also an authentic first-century winepress that they had excavated on the grounds, one that Jesus might well have known and observed in his growing years, and which later became an image in his teaching (Matt. 21:33). A bit farther up the slope was a building with replicas of the equipment used to crush olives into oil (something of which we'll have more to say when we come to the Garden of Gethsemane), and a wonderful example of a first-century synagogue. It was here, in a synagogue very much like this, that Jesus would have sat and listened to the reading of the Law, here that he would have heard the ringing words of the prophecies that pointed straight to him.

As we walked along the scrubby slope on which Nazareth Village is built, birds flitted here and there around us. Most of them were House Sparrows (I thought I saw a Shrike out of the corner of my eye, but it flew quickly away). Those sparrows, though one of the commonest birds in the world, must have also caught the eye of the young Jesus. He spoke about sparrows during his ministry, saying that "not one of them is forgotten by God" (Luke 12:6). There's even an ancient folktale about Jesus' childhood which includes a winsome, if somewhat fanciful, story about Jesus and the sparrows: it claims that the young Messiah so appreciated these birds that he would mold little sparrow-statuettes from clay and then clap his hands to make them come alive.

The second site in Nazareth connected to Jesus' childhood was back at the Basilica of the Annunciation, near where the center of the ancient village stood. In the lower level of that great cathedral, there's a spot that may be directly connected to Jesus' early years. The vast understory was dark in places, but brightly lit in others, giving an air of holiness and mystery all at the same time. We reverently circled the center of the lower level, where the footings of a Byzantine church still stood, and in the center was a broad, flat altar-table topped with a beautiful golden cross.

But it was the side-chapel just beside the great table that held everyone's interest. As we circled the lower level, we joined a line of pilgrims waiting to catch a glimpse. Norah explained what lay ahead, and a thrill ran through my heart. I had read about this in my guidebooks, and it was the portion of the church I most wanted to see: the remains of a first-century house that had been enshrined within the successive churches on this spot for millennia, the very house wherein the event of the annunciation may have taken place, and perhaps where Jesus would have spent his early years. Of course there's no way now to tell for certain if this was indeed the house where it all happened, but there was a good chance that the spot did lie somewhere within the grounds of that great church, and it was not without significance that this particular house had been preserved for all the ages.

As we drew near, we were able to peer through a small set of wrought iron gates into the house's interior. While some elements were clearly more recent—an altar and a pillar marking the purported locations of Mary and the angel—one could readily make out the ancient elements from the roughness of the old stonework around and behind. In the rear there was a little flight of worn stairs receding from the pillar, and it was easy to imagine the boy Jesus bounding up and down those stairs in youthful exuberance. Maybe they were steps he climbed every day, back and forth from his home to the workshop where he and Joseph labored in the sacred ministry of building good things for their neighbors.

While on that thought of Jesus as a carpenter, it's worth noting an old Palestinian remembrance about Jesus, coming from within just a couple generations of his life (from Justin Martyr, who had grown up near Galilee). This second-century anecdote says that Joseph and Jesus were known for their work in making wooden yokes and plows for oxen. This attests to their high level of skill: making yokes was precise and difficult work, since the yokes usually had to be specially fitted to each particular beast of burden. A good yoke, made according to the lines of an ox's frame, was comfortable and would enable the ox to pull well without tiring; but a second-rate yoke, or one made without specifications to the individual animal, would fit poorly and be painful. This little fact about one of Jesus' areas of expertise adds new depth to his famous invitation: "Take my yoke upon you and learn from me, for I am gentle and humble in heart, and you will find rest for your souls; for my yoke is easy, and my burden is light" (Matt. 11:29–30). Jesus, as a maker of yokes, knew what he was talking about. We were made to bear the yoke of Christ—he himself is the only thing in the universe that will fit the form of our fashioning. Any other yoke will burden us with pain and frustration, but following Jesus grants us the yoke of his peace.

After Jesus begins his work of preaching and healing, Nazareth features in the story only a couple more times, and never in a positive light. Matthew and Mark relate that Jesus does not work many miracles there, because of the people's lack of faith (Matt. 13:58; Mark 6:6). And Luke has Jesus launching his public ministry with a sermon in the Nazareth synagogue, in which he claims to be the fulfillment of Isaiah's prophecy of the messianic restoration (Luke 4:14–21; Is. 61). The crowd's first response is amazement, but it quickly turns to shock and rebuke when Jesus begins to challenge their long-held assumptions, proclaiming that the year of the Lord's favor will not be for the sole benefit of their clan, nor for their nation only, but will extend even to those beyond Israel's fold (Luke 4:22–30). The crowd's reaction is alarming: they are so enraged that they seize Jesus and take him to the edge of the ridge, ready to throw him down to his death.

Among many commentators, this wild overreaction is explained away as the anger of pious Jews who think they've heard blasphemy. But the crowd's response makes even more sense if the "royal clan" theory of Nazareth's settlement is true. If, indeed, these are people who have especially treasured Isaiah's prophecy, applied it to themselves and their destiny, and seen their own particular glory in its future fulfillment, then it would have been an assault on their highest hopes and dearest dreams to hear Jesus' message: that the messianic restoration would not be aimed at the exaltation of their long-suffering kingly clan, but rather extended out to unworthy Gentile sinners. And to have this shocking, repulsive interpretation preached by one of their own—it may have been too much to take. They would have seen Jesus as an apostate to their legacy, as a dangerous false preacher who could bring shame down on the family line if he was permitted to go forward with his ministry.

But whatever motivated their anger, it didn't matter in the end. It could not stand against the authority of God's Messiah, nor subvert his sovereign plan. The drama ends with a conclusion so anticlimactic as to be startling: Jesus simply walks out of the middle of the mob, and goes on his way. The world may not want to hear the message Jesus brings; it may even resist with anger, threats, and violence; but it will never have power to stop that message, nor to silence its call.

BRIDGES OF FAITH AND LOVE

Jesus shall reign where'er the sun
Does its successive journeys run;
His Kingdom stretch from shore to shore,
Till moons shall wax and wane no more.

—Isaac Watts, "Jesus Shall Reign"

In all four Gospels, the first narrative of Christ as an adult is the story of how he appeared in the middle of John the Baptist's ministry at the Jordan River. Matthew, Mark, and Luke go a bit further than John, and relate the story of Jesus' baptism at John's hands. On our tour, we visited two different baptismal sites on the Jordan, with the more southerly one, not far from Jericho, claiming the more ancient tradition of being the place of Jesus' baptism. To get there, we drove into the West Bank, following the downward path of the river as it plunged ever farther below sea level, down into the depths of the desert's crucible.

When one travels in the West Bank—a territory officially held by Israel but with portions of it governed by the Palestinian Authority—one is confronted with the stark reality of the Holy Land's divided life. The Palestinians—largely Muslim, but with an ancient and enduring Christian minority—live every day with the hardness of boundaries and walls and armed soldiers as part of their reality. The Israelis, too, for their part, wrestle with how best to live in a bitterly divided land. Sometimes boundaries represent oppression; sometimes they represent prudence; and sometimes the balance between the two is tremendously hard to determine. But whatever one's opinion might be of the division of the Holy Land, one cannot but be struck by the simple, disheartening fact that it is divided.

When we stopped at the baptismal site on the lower Jordan, division was one of the evident themes. The river is a border, and the separation is clear. On one side, the West Bank, and on the other, the Hashemite Kingdom of Jordan. As we walked down to the riverbank beneath an unforgiving sun, I paused to look around. Here, amid the broiling heat and the brown hills and the water sluicing through the rushes, Christ had stepped into the water to follow his Father's call.

One of the questions that always arises from the story of Jesus' baptism is why he had to be baptized at all. John was preaching a baptism of repentance, so if Jesus was sinless, why would he need to undergo this ritual? In writing his Gospel, Matthew may have been aware of this tension, because he records John the Baptist asking Jesus a similar question: "I need to be baptized by you, and do you come to me?" Jesus' answer is confident, but enigmatic: "Let it be so now; it is proper to do this to fulfill all righteousness" (Matt. 3:13–15).

But what exactly was Jesus fulfilling? There have been lots of interpretations offered over the years, and many of them are compelling. Perhaps Jesus was simply undertaking baptisim as a ritual of consecration before he began his ministry, or demonstrating in this physical way that John the Baptist was indeed his forerunner. Or perhaps it was intended to mirror the ablutions and immersions used by priests when they began their consecrated service. This, coupled with a divine anointing by the descent of the Holy Spirit, may point to a visible demonstration of Jesus' office as the great High Priest and the true King of Israel.

The baptism may also be intended as the fulfillment of Old Testament foreshadowings. One possibility is that it mirrors Israel's experience of passing through the Red Sea—they were led by God through the waters to freedom, and Jesus now also leads us through the waters of baptism to freedom from sin. Here's another one: just as Joshua led the children of Israel through the Jordan River to inherit their Promised Land, so too the new Joshua (which would be the Hebrew version of Jesus' name) goes through the Jordan to open the way for his people's salvation. All of these possibilities strike me as harmonious interpretations of the passage. As with many parts of Scripture, this may not be a black-and-white decision ("Jesus' baptism means this, but not that"); rather, it may be better to read the Gospel accounts in the same way we listen to a classical symphony, where we expect to find multiple themes weaving together in perfect harmony.

One of these fulfillment stories particularly captures my imagination. It may be that Jesus' baptism is a reenactment of Creation. It's easy to see a number of immediate parallels between the baptism story and the Creation account of Genesis 1: the voice of God the Father speaking; the Son of God also present, who is the Word by which all things were made; and the Spirit descending over the waters. Even God's pronouncement over Jesus, "with him I am well pleased," carries echoes of Genesis 1: "he saw that it was good." And the parallels don't stop there. When Jesus tells John, "let it be so now," he uses a grammatical construction that calls the Creation story to mind. Where he could have simply said, "Do it," instead he says, "Let it be," just as God said, "Let there be light." Perhaps Jesus' reason for being baptized, "to fulfill all righteousness," ought to be understood in the sense of "setting all things at right." Eugene Peterson paraphrases the verse in precisely this way in *The Message*: "God's work, putting things right all these centuries, is coming together right now in this baptism."

If the baptism is, among other things, a nod to the Creation account, then it becomes a beautiful picture of God's intention to restore his Creation. Essentially, it is an announcement that the great project of New Creation is launching here and now, through the person of Jesus Christ. Whereas we, by our sin, ruptured our intended unity with God, now Jesus will bring it all back together again. Where there was division between us and God, Jesus would bring reconciliation. And this project of bringing unity in the restored Creation extends not just to our relationship with God, but encompasses all things, as Paul testifies in Eph. 1:10: "to bring unity to all things in heaven and on earth under Christ."

And there, at the River Jordan, I saw a world desperately in need of the unity Christ brings.

———·———

I was struck by a few things as I looked around the scene. First, the Jordan River was shockingly small. I knew this would be the case, but I hadn't realized just how starkly the water had diminished. It used to be a proper river—indeed, a river too wide to cross without finding a ford of some sort. But the water-usage demands of modern nation-states have sucked the Jordan's watershed nearly dry, and all that remains at the base of the river is something we could barely call a stream. Joshua and the children of Israel wouldn't have needed a miracle from God to cross this water: all they would have to do is throw down a couple wooden planks and they could make it across without wetting their feet. The Jordan was little more than a lazy, muddy trickle, winding its way through a bed of rushes as it approached the languid stillness of the Dead Sea.

The other thing that struck me was the border. I live in a border town in the US, and we have to go through the rigmarole of passports and customs checks as a simple part of daily life; nevertheless, it feels like we're part of the same community as our Canadian neighbors across the river, with just a bit of bureaucratic annoyance in the middle. Here, though, it wasn't just a matter of a bridge with some customs booths: the river itself was divided in two. On the far bank lay Jordan, one of the Muslim-majority kingdoms crafted out of the wreckage of the Ottoman Empire. And here was Israel, home of the Palestinians, the Jews, and the borderland realities of the West Bank. And in the middle was a rope that marked off the sides, so that no one could cross.

There was a strange sort of irony in this. Here, in the very place that Jesus waded through the waters to begin his ministry, coming together with his kinsman-forerunner, and in the very place where the divine dove of peace alighted upon him, now there stood an open symbol of division. But that wasn't the whole story. You see, on the other side of that rope border in the river sat a row of Jordanian Christians, smiling across the way at us as their feet dangled in the water. They, like us, were there at that spot out of love for Christ. And we, though separated by an imaginary line that someone had drawn on a map long ago, were united to them in heart and in spirit. Here were our brothers and sisters. Above them, farther up the bank, stood a magnificent church, and behind that, a Christian monastery. Immediately, a snippet of Scripture flashed through my mind: "For he himself is our peace, who has made the two groups one and has destroyed the barrier, the dividing wall of hostility... Consequently, you are no longer foreigners and strangers, but fellow citizens with God's people and members of his household" (Eph. 2:14, 19).

Despite the outward appearance of the river, split by boundaries that keep men apart, Christ had indeed "destroyed the barrier." To me, a Christian, that far bank was as much my home as the near bank was, because my family lived on both. Rather than feeling separated from those Jordanian Christians, I felt an instant flash of kinship's fondness toward them. The border became little more than a mirage; for I had bridges of faith and love that could reach beyond it. I was a citizen of the kingdom of God, a kingdom without borders or walls. Jesus had done something there, in that small corner of the world that we call Israel, which had let every race become my brothers and every land my home.

THE CALL OF
THE ASCETIC WAY

Tarry no longer; toward thine heritage
Haste on thy way, and be of right good cheer.
Go each day onward on thy pilgrimage;
Think how short a time thou hast abiden here.

—John Lydgate, "Vox ultima Crucis"

Aﬆer our stop at the Jordan River, we took our lunch at a restaurant in Jericho, pausing to rest in the shade and to wolf down the marvelous delights of shawarma sandwiches. To all appearances, Jericho was a Muslim city now, with the minarets of mosques stretching skyward on every side. But I knew that we were now entering the heartland of ancient Christian Palestine: the Judean Desert between Jerusalem and the river valley, where countless saints had poured out their lives in the ministry of prevailing prayer. Even Jericho, featured in Scripture as the site of Joshua's conquest and Jesus' ministry encounters, had a long but oft-forgotten history of ascetic faith. Many abbas and ammas—the desert fathers and desert mothers of early Christian history—had taken the hills around that city as the place of their labors.

One of my favorites was Chariton the Confessor, who had first come to the area of Jericho as a pilgrim. He was set upon by bandits, kidnapped, and held prisoner in their cave. Some time afterward, the bandits met an untimely end, and Chariton, now free and in possession of their treasure trove, decided to give away their plunder to the poor. More than that, he interpreted the painful experience of capture as God's providence in his life, and so he took the place of his trauma—the cave in which he had been held—and resolved to make it a place from which God's blessing could pour forth. So he became a hermit-monk, spending the rest of his life in and around that cave, patiently giving his time to great labors of prayer, Bible study, and Christian counsel. His story reminded me of an Lilias Trotter quote: "Take the very hardest thing in your life, the place of difficulty, outward or inward, and expect God to triumph gloriously in that very spot. Just there he can bring your soul into blossom." One of my great desires, during my pilgrimage and on many other days of my life, was to have God do precisely that.

———·———

We were headed that day into the blistering heat of the Judean Desert, just as Jesus, after his baptism, had retreated into the wilderness to fast and to pray. The aim of our day's journey was a glimpse into the world of asceticism—the rigor of devotional practices like prayer, fasting, and Scripture study undertaken by the proto-monastic Jews at Qumran.

In the Gospels, we are thrown into the story of the wilderness temptations at the climax of Jesus' time of fasting. He has already been out there forty days, and then the tempter comes. Satan tries three times to entice Jesus to sin, to waver in his resolution to follow the way his Father has set for him, but each time Jesus stands firm. One of the interesting features of the temptation story is that it fits the interwoven themes of several strands of Old Testament fulfillment that we noted at Jesus' baptism. If the baptism was a reenactment of Creation, then it's no surprise that the next scene includes a confrontation with the tempter. But where Adam and Eve succumbed to Satan's suggestions, Jesus rebukes him. The New Creation will not be thrown off course like the old one was, because now it is God in the flesh who has come to set it right. Similarly, if the baptism was a mirroring of Israel passing through the Red Sea, then it's no surprise that Jesus immediately goes and spends forty days in the desert, just as Israel spent forty years in the desert before entering the Promised Land.

Ascetic practices, like Jesus' fasting, are often misunderstood (especially in my tradition, where potluck dinners are much more a regular feature than fasting is). I recently joined my Catholic brother-in-law in a few months of attempting some ascetic practices, like fasting, regular prayer times, abstaining from entertainment media, and (the hardest one of all) cold showers. When I told people I was doing this, the most common response was something along the lines of, "Why on earth would you do that?" Unfortunately, that response shows just how far away we've gotten from a biblical understanding of ascetic practice. Most Protestants view monastic discipline and asceticism through the lens of medieval Catholic culture, in which such works were sometimes twisted into vain attempts to earn favor with God or to atone for one's sins through sheer misery. But that's not how the early Christian church understood ascetic practices.

The Greek word for asceticism, *askesis*, denotes "training" or "exercise." Just like you would keep your body healthy by exercising regularly, you are called to keep your soul healthy by regular spiritual disciplines. In the tradition in which I was raised, this usually amounted to a strong emphasis on reading my Bible and praying, both of which are absolutely indispensable. But what about other biblical disciplines, like fasting? The early church thought fasting was tremendously important for many reasons, and one of them was that it served as a way to discipline the body's urges, to train oneself to be able to say "no" to the flesh even at the moment of its sharpest desires. As Paul says, "I strike a blow to my body and make it my slave" (1 Cor. 9:27).

Fasting isn't just about food, you see. It's a training program that helps you to order your desires and direct your life, as empowered by the Holy Spirit, ever more in conformity with the way of God's holiness. If you have persevered in regular fasting, you will be less likely to give in to lust, greed, or anger when those natural urges come upon you in full force, because you've trained yourself how to say no to your body. Early Christians understood very well that humans are holistic beings—with a bodily and a spiritual nature, each intimately connected to the other—so we need to keep both in good working order together, lest one run feral. In this way, even weird disciplines like my (brief) practice of taking cold showers might have some benefit, if done in the right way and with the prayerful hope that God would use it to train me into a greater capacity for godly discipline. To quote Paul again: "Train yourself to be godly. For physical training has some value, but godliness has value for all things.... That is why we labor and strive...." (1 Tim. 4:7–10).

———·———

At Qumran, within the crown of hills that encircles the Dead Sea, lay the ruins of an ancient settlement, where a small sect of Jews had banded together to pursue a radically ascetic life. The desert was hot and fierce, but it offered a sort of purity, away from the world, that drew them to face its rigors. Like John the Baptist, with whom they were contemporaries, the Essenes of Qumran made the wilderness their home and devoted themselves to pursuing the will of God, as instructed by their interpretation of Scripture. It is thanks to their efforts that the priceless manuscript hoard known as the Dead Sea Scrolls has come down to us, confirming much of what we believed and enlightening much of what we came to learn about the Hebrew Bible and the Judaism of Jesus' day. Though not a site associated with any biblical story, Qumran now holds a place of honor in biblical history because of the legacy of faith and scholarship that it left us through the Dead Sea Scrolls.

We rode down into the bleak wasteland of the Dead Sea (a place we would come to see more fully later on), and by the time we stepped out of the bus at Qumran the heat had climbed so high that it was almost difficult to breathe. While there was a small air-conditioned visitor center there, most of our time was spent outdoors, making me grateful for the wide-brimmed Indiana Jones hat I was sporting. I'm sure it made me look very much like a typical American tourist, but that was a better fate than heatstroke.

We walked through the remains of the Qumran commune, marveling at the depth of the cisterns they had to use to survive in that blistering heat. Scattered all around us in the hills were the caves where the Dead Sea Scrolls had been hidden away nearly two millennia ago, until they finally came to light— by sheer accident (or providence)—in the middle of the twentieth century.

Of course, my eye was also drawn by the birds of Qumran, knowing that any species I found there would be unlikely to live anywhere else on earth. And remarkably, there were a few birds well-adapted enough to survive there: I saw the lean, dark form of a Blackstart, the swooping flight of Rock Martins and Crag Martins, and the distant orange-and-black flash of a Tristram's Starling. It takes a special kind of bird to live in a place like that, and it may just take a special sort of person to devote oneself to a life of ascetic spiritual disciplines. (Isn't it a telling sign of our culture's priorities that we laud body-focused athletes to the apex of celebrity, but pay no heed to the great spiritual athletes in our midst?) I'm not sure that I want to be an ascetic in the full sense of a monastic vocation, but I want to *be able* to be an ascetic, if that makes any sense. I often felt like I didn't even have a single scrap of the discipline that would be required to make a go of it, and I yearned to find just a bit of perseverant resolve in my daily life.

The truth is, I wouldn't ever trade the delights of God's blessings in my family and my work for a stern and celibate asceticism, but the inspiration of ancient monks has often been a spur in my side that presses me toward walking in greater holiness. And to stand there, in the place where Christianity's vast monastic tradition was foreshadowed, in the hills that Christ himself knew—it was an honor and a thrill. The great task of holiness that they had been engaged in two thousand years ago: it was my great pilgrimage too. It was already my inheritance through the work of Christ, already empowered by the Holy Spirit, and now, by God's providence, I had the honor of walking the road he had laid out for me: to live a godly life (2 Pet. 1:3).

NEW JOY WHEN
WE'VE RUN DRY

There was some one thing that was too great for
God to show us when he walked upon our earth;
and I have sometimes fancied that it was his mirth.

—G. K. Chesterton, *Orthodoxy*

After his time in the wilderness, Jesus begins his public ministry. The Gospel of John includes a story that fits somewhere
in this period: Jesus' attendance at the wedding in Cana. There are
several possibilities for this location, so it numbers among those
many sites in the Holy Land of which we're just not sure if this
is exactly where Jesus performed his works. But it might well be.
Roman Catholic and Eastern Orthodox churches mark adjacent
sites in Cana as the location of the Savior's famous act of turning
the water into wine. The town itself is just a few miles down the

road from Nazareth, which makes good sense of the fact that Jesus and his family appear to be friends of the groom.

To get to the churches of Cana today, one needs to navigate a rather bewildering array of old cobblestone alleys. Even our guide needed to refresh her bearings once or twice to get us there. Once we arrived, we squeezed into the courtyard of the Catholic church. Not only was it a bit tighter than the spacious courts of Nazareth's basilica, but this site was also thronged with massive groups of pilgrims. Once again I was struck by the reality of the vast global fellowship of the Body of Christ—worshipers from many different nations, all brought together by their united love for the Savior from Galilee. This site appeared to attract a tremendous number of Ethiopian Christians, for whom (I'm told) the story of the wedding at Cana has a special resonance.

There was a celebratory air to the throng gathered there; I saw many smiles in Cana. It seemed like an echo of that first celebration still clung to the air, even two thousand years later. In my work on my Gospel poetry project that year, I had the experience (as often happens) of a line coming to me as if out of the blue: in telling the story of Cana, there wasn't quite enough substance from John's account to fill out one of the lines, and I needed a few more beats, a phrase that could complete the previous rhyme. All of the sudden, a certain description of Jesus and his friends popped into my head: "They laughed and they sang." I had never before imagined Jesus as laughing and singing— even though I always pictured him as full of love, he also had an unshakable, otherworldly composure in my mind's eye. But he was at a Jewish wedding, a celebration of the love of his friends; of course he laughed and sang! That realization, connected to the story of Cana, helped fill out my understanding of Jesus' full human nature.

We walked first into one of the adjoining courtyards, looking for a quieter spot to have our little mini-service before we entered the church. We gathered in a nook beside the shade of a lemon tree, and there went through our comfortable little liturgy: one participant would do a recitation of the Gospel story, and we would all sing a song together. Here, though, there was an added element: an option to do a "renewing of the vows" for any married couples in the group, in honor of Christ's celebration of marriage at that very spot. So we had a lovely little service for one of our older couples, members of Josh's church, and it was, I think, a deeply meaningful experience for them. (Incidentally, I much appreciated Josh's decision to phrase it as a "reaffirmation" of their vows rather than a "renewing," for the very simple reason that marriage vows don't expire.) I thought of my wife and wished, not for the first time, that she could have been there with me—not that it would have been either sensible or practical to have us both there in our current circumstances, but simply that I missed her.

My wife once told me about a wedding homily she had heard, which used the story of Jesus at Cana, and it's one that I now come back to each time I do a wedding. It serves as a valuable reminder that we need to rely on the grace of Christ in our families and our marriages. You see, the "honeymoon period" of early marriage is wonderful and intoxicating, just like the season of plentiful wine at the beginning of Cana's wedding. But that wine runs out eventually. Feelings will change or fade a bit, the daily grind of humdrum routine will intrude on our relationships, and responsibilities will stack up and leave us with little left to give to one another. Sometimes, couples are shocked to find that the wineskins of their romance have run completely dry, and all they are left with is plain old water. But with Christ as the center of our relationships, water can be turned into wine. He can guide us through the hard times, and, in the end, give back to us overflowing casks of new wine, better even than the first.

To close our visit, we did a quick circuit around the church of Cana. It was interesting, but not among the more remarkable churches we visited in Israel. The one significant point of interest was that they had an authentic first-century water container there, of the same sort described in the Gospel story, which had been excavated from that very site. It's not necessarily an indication that the site is authentic, since such containers were among the commonest of items in the ancient world, but it was a fascinating connection to the story nonetheless. That story, of the empty wineskins replaced with water-jars now brimming with the best of wines at the word of the Lord, has always reminded me that we serve a God who can take our emptiness and fill us up with his goodness in ways we cannot even imagine.

THE VIEW FROM
THE MOUNTAIN

O Sabbath rest of Galilee,
O calm of hills above!—
Where Jesus knelt to share with Thee
The silence of eternity,
Interpreted by love.

—John Greenleaf Whittier, "Dear Lord and Father of Mankind"

After the wedding at Cana and Nazareth's furious rejection of Jesus following his sermon in the synagogue, he moved on to take up residence near the Sea of Galilee. The road would have led him eastward, out of the central hills, around the base of Mount Arbel, and out onto the shores of the lake. (The Sea of Galilee, though referenced in various ways in the Gospels, is in fact a landlocked, freshwater lake, and I'll be referring to it as both sea and lake throughout the next few chapters.)

One of the most delightful excursions we had in Galilee was up the slope of Mount Arbel. That mountain was one of the most pleasantly jarring shake-ups to the way I had always imagined Galilee. In my mind's eye, I had seen it as a place of gentle slopes and rolling hills—and in some places it is—but I never knew that right there, along the shoreline that Christ called home during his ministry, he would have looked up to see the craggy, charismatic wonder of Mount Arbel every day, with its sharp edges, high cliff faces, and blanket of shadows and caves.

After enjoying our hotel's breakfast buffet, we all loaded up into Najji's silver bus and drove off to the walking trails on Mount Arbel. The mountain would be quite an arduous climb if approached from the cliffs that faced the lake, but thankfully it has a fairly gentle ascent on its other side, complete with a drivable road that takes one up to within a mile of the peak. I was very excited about this site, mostly for obvious reasons (birds!), but also because it offered a connection with part of Jesus' story that had always resonated with me: at many points in the Gospels, Jesus, weary from his ministry labors, withdraws by himself up to a mountain to pray. For me, a representative of that most classic of tragic archetypes—the introvert trying to do an extra-vert's job—I connected deeply with this practice of Jesus. In those stories, I felt that I understood his experience and could relate to his feelings. So to be there, on one of the mountains of the lake, taking in the view that Christ saw while he was praying and renewing his energy for another day of ministry—it gave a sweet sense of closeness to my Lord.

In our American culture, we put a great deal of emphasis on our work. We even define ourselves by our work, offering up information about our jobs as a way to get to know one another. But we don't give much attention to rest. (Now, truth be told, many of us sometimes face the opposite problem, and give a lot of time to resting, but our culture hardwires us to feel bad about it, because we know that work is the thing we're supposed to be doing.) We even raise our children in the hope that they will be "productive members of soci-ety," as if producing something was the height of one's value in life. The fact that Jesus so intentionally and so often took time to rest should give us a hint that there's something a little bit off in our priorities.

A couple years ago, I was flipping through an art book, and stumbled across a painting by the French artist James Tissot. It showed Jesus speaking to his disciples, who were sitting on a rocky hillside, and the painting was titled

"Jesus Commands His Disciples to Rest." I was pretty familiar with the Gospel stories that are usually depicted in paintings, and this one came as a surprise. I wasn't even sure at first if it was a real Gospel story. I knew that Jesus rested, but I couldn't remember him commanding his disciples to rest. So I looked up the verse to which the title referred, and sure enough, there it was: "Come with me by yourselves to a quiet place and get some rest" (Mark 6:31). We, too, are his disciples. We, too, are commanded to come away with him and rest.

But it's important to understand that rest, in the biblical sense, is meant to be restorative. The way we rest in our society isn't always like that. It usually bounces to one of two extremes: either vacations so jam-packed with places to see and things to do that we end up exhausted by the time we're home; or sitting on our couches, eating junk food, watching TV, and scrolling social media until our brains ooze out of our ears. Too often, our "rest" leaves us either exhausted or empty.

That's not the biblical idea of rest. It's meant to be a time to restore both body and soul, to gain strength and to commune with God. Even our word "recreation" tells the tale of this biblical idea, because it's actually the word "re-creation." In our rest and recreation, we are making space for God's work of re-creation in our hearts, bodies, and minds. So, like Jesus, let's retreat to the mountain, drink in the beauty of our world, and rest our souls in the radiance of God's love.

———·———

We took to the trail, following Norah across the gentle incline as it wove through a field of brush and grass. And here, in a different habitat than the ones I had already encountered, I started to see a wide array of birds: the indigo flash of a Blue Rock Thrush on one side, and on the other the zebra-striped flight of the sherbet-orange hoopoe. I also saw one of the species I had been hoping to find, a common Old World bird: the Great Tit. It was a European representative of one of my favorite families of birds, the much-beloved chickadees of my home. And, in fact, these birds looked very much like chickadees, just a little bigger and a little yellower, but bobbing around from flower to bush in the friendly and energetic way that seemed so familiar to me from watching their New World cousins.

As we walked, Norah indicated some of the points of interest, including the mustard plants that Jesus referred to more than once in his parables and analogies. Flowers bloomed on every side and bright sunshine washed over us as we made our way to the crest of the mountain. Once there, we could look out over the whole scope of the valley to our left and the lake to our right (though unfortunately the day was warm enough that a haze over the water made it difficult to get a good view in that direction). The road in the valley below us, Norah explained, marked the route of the old Roman road in Jesus' time, and it was probably that very road that led him down from Nazareth to the Sea of Galilee when he was just beginning his ministry. I tried to picture him walking down there, with these great towers of stone on either side, but I found it rather difficult to imagine what he must have been feeling as he saw the shining waters of Gennesaret appear before him.

While I was thinking of this, I happened to notice another little bird perched out on a branch on a nearby part of the cliff face. I recognized it immediately, even though it was another new species for me: one that I had been looking for, a European Goldfinch. Here again was a cousin of one of my familiar favorites back in Maine, the American Goldfinch, bright and flashy in its brilliant saffron coat. The European variety is not quite so eye-catching in color, except that it has a prominent splash of red right in the center of its face. Interestingly, this bird has a long connection with the story of Jesus: old European legends told how its red face came from a drop of blood at the crucifixion. Even the goldfinches' scientific names remind one that old story— carduelis ("thistle") in Europe, calling to mind Christ's crown of thorns, and tristis ("sad") in America. As I watched this bird on Mount Arbel, it actually looked sad. There was a strange heaviness to its manner; its head bowing reflectively every now and then.

I had just been wondering about how Jesus felt as he journeyed down from Nazareth to Capernaum to start his ministry, and maybe here was part of the answer: perhaps amid all the excitement of the mission ahead of him, all the love and joy and peace that flowed so constantly from his presence, there was also a touch of mourning already there. The Gospels show that he knew where the end of this road of ministry would take him. Perhaps he already had in mind the sacrifice that these steps would lead him toward. Or perhaps he was still thinking about his leave-taking from Nazareth, when the offended neighbors of his old hometown nearly threw him off a cliff. In any case, it was striking to find this reminder of the sorrows of Christ perched right over the spot where I had conjectured about his emotions, a reminder of the richly complex human experience that our Savior shared with us.

DARING TO FOLLOW FULLY

The healing of His seamless dress
Is by our beds of pain;
We touch Him in life's throng and press,
And we are whole again.

—John Greenleaf Whittier, "Our Master"

One of the most interesting archaeological sites we visited was
the excavation at Migdal (or, in the language of the Gospels,
Magdala). Magdala was, of course, the hometown of Mary Magdalene, and it lay just a ways down the shore from Capernaum
and near where Jesus would have reached the Sea of Galilee after
leaving Nazareth. It was here, along these shorelines from Migdal
to Bethsaida, that Jesus would begin calling his disciples.

I've often wondered what sort of person Mary Magdalene
was—there's not a lot about her personality in the Gospels, save

that she was deeply devoted to Christ. Various and contradictory threads about her exist within Christian traditions: the Western tradition often thinks of her as a prostitute or adulteress who, after meeting Christ, lived a life of godly penitence; but the Eastern (and probably older) tradition simply sees her as a woman who had been tragically afflicted by demonic attacks in her early life, was delivered by Christ as the Gospels relate, and then followed him as one of the most faithful and commendable of his early circle of disciples. But whichever way you read it, hers is a story of deliverance from an old life and then a new life filled with love and devotion to Christ. In that, she is a figure whom I have always found deeply sympathetic: I've often longed for dramatic deliverances from my own failings, and I've also yearned to be able to walk consistently in the simple faithfulness of following Christ. Hers is a story of radical transformation: from brokenness and desperate need, to becoming "the apostle to the apostles," the first witness of Christ's resurrection (John 20:1–18).

The site of her hometown is rich in both peace and personality—it boasts two sanctuaries, one from Jesus' day and one from our own, which both breathe a spirit of peace; and it is thronged with some of the most interesting, charismatic, and assertive birds I encountered in Israel. We paused first at the old sanctuary: the remains of a first-century synagogue where Jesus would have taught (Matt. 4:23). Our tour guide had us reach in and place a hand on the stone seats around the edge, as if we were claiming a spot for ourselves to sit and listen to Jesus. Maybe it was in or around that very synagogue that Mary Magdalene first met her Lord.

We surveyed the ruins of the town, which were extensive and interesting, including elaborate systems for processing fish and preparing them for market, ritual baths for purity laws, and mosaics in the homes of the wealthier residents. But of equal interest to me were the current residents of the town: it appeared to be the territory of a gang of Spur-winged Lapwings, the cocky and assertive cousins of our sandpipers and plovers. They're odd-looking and beautiful in equal measure, and they kept a very close eye on us as we paraded through their village toward the new sanctuary, the Catholic pilgrimage church called "Duc in Altem."

Just before we entered the church, something caught my eye: a flurry of motion in the sky ahead, where two lapwings were flapping up to challenge an interloper who had suddenly soared into the scene. It only took me a moment to make the identification, because it was the bird I had been most hoping to see in Israel: a Eurasian Kestrel, the Old World counterpart to my favorite bird of all, the American Kestrel. As I mentioned back in the first Nazareth chapter, I had come to associate kestrels with my sense of God's calling. Specifically, they represented God's invitation to go deeper, to answer him with courage, abandon, and reckless faith. Kestrels had come to speak to me, in the "sign language" that God speaks to us in unforeseen moments, as a dare to throw off my restraints and give everything to pursuing a life of vibrant holiness. And there, in the sky over the Sea of Galilee, where Christ had called his own disciples, I saw God's daring invitation dart across the sky again.

We stepped through the doorways of the Duc in Altem church and took in the scene. The sanctuary was broad and full of sunlight, looking out over the Sea of Galilee through wide glass panels. The interior was lined with beautiful golden icons, and the stage itself, with the pulpit and altar, was in the shape of a first-century fishing boat. The atrium, fashioned out of lovely pink granite, was an homage to Mary Magdalene and the other women of faith who form the core of Christianity's story, but who are too often overlooked by history and tradition. Little side-chapels illustrated some of the powerful moments of Jesus' story in that area, and particularly his calling and deliverance of Mary Magdalene and the other disciples. This church, with its thoughtful intentionality, became a favorite site for many of the women in our group.

Down a small set of steps was one more chapel, set directly on the stones of the old first-century village road. The altarpiece was a broad, beautiful painting of the moment when the bleeding woman reached out to touch the hem of Jesus' robe. This chapel, set on the very stones where Jesus likely would have walked, was set aside for those who wanted a place to pray and encounter him as that woman did: a gracious Savior who responds with mercy to our outstretched cry for healing. It fit exactly with my feelings and hopes for my time in Israel. My glimpse of the kestrel, and God's call to courageous following, struck me as an echo of what I had experienced in Jesus' own hometown: praying for healing, and seeing a sign of encouragement and invitation of God daring me to follow him with abandon.

It wasn't until after I returned home that I discovered what "Duc in Altem" means. It comes from the story of Jesus' call to Peter by the shore. In that encounter, Jesus presents his challenge to Peter by encouraging him to fish one more time, and he does this by saying, "Put out into the deep" (or in Latin, "duc in altem"). What an invitation: put out into the deep, cast off the bowlines that tie you to the shore, and go out adventuring on the waves. Those words spoke Christ's call to me, as I had written their invitation down many years ago in an old poem:

Come, and follow.
Come and follow, and I'll open for you
A new world, a new life,
A resurrection that will make you sing
With all the power of the breaking dawn.
Freedom is yours, and life is yours—
All you must do is follow, and believe.
The Kingdom awaits your choice, my son—
Step out into the tempest of living,
And I will make you truly alive.

A RESTING PLACE
FOR MY SOUL

Him evermore I behold
Walking in Galilee,
Through the cornfield's waving gold,
In hamlet or in grassy wold,
By the shores of the Beautiful Sea.

—Henry Wadsworth Longfellow, "I Heard Him Call"

A t this point, it's worth pausing for a few moments to consider the scene before us: the Sea of Galilee, that broad and beautiful theater-in-the-round where so much of the drama of Jesus' ministry took place. The lake is about thirteen miles long and eight miles wide, and ringed by hills on most of its sides. It goes by many different names in the Bible: Sea of Galilee, Sea of Tiberas, Chinnereth, and Gennesaret. Of its many towns mentioned in the Gospels, only Tiberias has survived all the way into the twenty-first century as a living city. And while it's simply a large lake, in many ways like any other lake, there is something wondrous about it. When I started my pilgrimage, I expected the journey to be interesting and exciting, but I didn't expect to develop sentimental attachments to the places I visited. And yet, there by the waters of Gennesaret, I did.

We were lodged at a hotel on the grounds of a kibbutz along the northwestern shore of the lake. At the end of our first day there, as our happy band of pilgrims trudged wearily back to the comfort of their rooms, I set out to look for birds by the last light of evening. A little path led me down beside a trickling stream, beneath the towering forms of high trees, and then out beside a sea-grass marsh that flanked the waters of the lake. I was stunned at how good the birding was: just on the hotel grounds alone, there was a broad swath of rich, varied habitats: a stream, a marsh, a lake, a pebbled beach, tall trees, low bushes, well-groomed lawns, and adjoining fields of both short and long grasses. It would not be stretching it to call it a birding paradise, especially since I happened to be there during the magical days of the spring migration. On that very first night I started racking up line after line of new species for my life list: various kinds of egrets and herons and gulls and cormorants that I had never seen before, and other birds for which I did not even have a reference in my experience of birding in Maine: lapwings, parakeets, sunbirds, and wagtails.

Faced with the lapping waters of the Sea of Galilee, I did as I had done in the Mediterranean: slipped off my shoes and socks, rolled up my pants, and waded into the shallows. I couldn't help but smile, thinking of how many times Jesus had probably rolled up the hem of his garments, just like me, to step out and climb into Peter's boat.

When I think about the Sea of Galilee, and the role that it played in the Gospels, two stories immediately take center-stage: Jesus calming the storm, and Jesus walking on the water. During our stay by the lake, we got the chance to go out on a boat and see the surrounding countryside from out upon the waves. Our boat was big and bulky, designed for tourist trips, and we had the benefit of bright skies and calm winds. But it wasn't hard to imagine what it must have felt like, out there on the water in a much smaller boat, when the clash of weather systems at the edge of the hills sent furious winds whipping down at the lake. Such storms, I'm told, do happen on the Sea of Galilee from time to time, and it was in just such a storm that the disciples were caught, and feared that they were lost.

On the wall of my church office, I have a print of one of Rembrandt's paintings, "Christ in the Storm on the Sea of Galilee." It's full of wild and violent motion: the boat is surging up and listing to the side at the same time, riding the slope of a whitecap. One of the disciples is desperately pulling at the tiller, others are tugging at the sail, clinging to the mast, or slumped over in despair, and still others are pleading with Jesus. Christ himself, still lying down near the stern, looks back at his disciples with an expression full of calm authority. In the next moment, the Gospels tell us, he will stand up in the heaving boat, and command the waters to be still. When the wind and waters obey Jesus, and everything settles into a quiet, sudden calm, the disciples are struck with "fear and amazement" (Luke 8:25). And no wonder, after witnessing such a raw display of divine power. There could be no mistaking what had happened, nor what it meant about Jesus. In the Old Testament Scriptures, it was God alone who held the power to tame the sea (Ps. 65:7; 89:9; 107:29).

The story of Jesus walking on the water is no less astonishing than his calming of the storm, and the disciples react to it with the same kind of terrified wonder that any mortal human would. It is another display of Jesus' power over the sea, a dreaded symbol of primeval chaos in the minds of many Jews. And yet despite the power of the sea, despite the power of any danger, God's power is always greater.

Jesus' act of walking on the water might also be an implicit claim to his divine kingship. Ancient writers would sometimes criticize the vain pretensions of pompous kings by saying that they believed they could walk on water. In fact, that was the very barb that 2 Maccabees 5:21 aimed at the wicked king Antiochus in the second century BC: "he thought in his arrogance that he could sail on the land and walk on the sea." Antiochus had called himself "Epiphanes"—"God Manifest"—and every godly Jew knew the story of his unhinged claims to divinity. And yet here came Jesus, doing the very thing that Antiochus was mocked for believing he could do. The claim may well have hit home among the disciples: here indeed, in Jesus of Nazareth, is God made manifest, walking in our midst.

In each of these stories, the gentle and awesome grace of our Lord meets the disciples' fear and failings and overcomes them all with the authority his presence. He truly is God made manifest, who reigns sovereign over all other powers. Any storm that may rise, he has power to calm. Many times we are afraid of being pulled down and lost in the cruel waves of suffering and sin, but the Master who once had power to quiet the storm still has that power today. And I—sinful I—could learn to walk the waves in victory and trust, if only I walked those waves with him.

In our stay at the Sea of Galilee, we didn't see any storms. It was peaceful, and that peace seemed to sink down into my soul. And on top of that peace, I was granted the wonder of drinking in the beauty of God's works in sunrises, mountains, and wildlife. As my poetic rendering of John 1:16 says, "Grace upon grace received we from him; yes, grace upon grace, and then grace again!"

Our first morning at the lake, I woke up more than an hour before breakfast, while my fellow pilgrims wisely opted to get enough sleep to carry them through the coming day. But the thrill of birding in a new place by the light of dawn drew me with intoxicating anticipation. I had studied my field guides and memorized a few of the calls of certain species I was looking for; and when I slipped out into the gray, pre-dawn light and heard the trilling of a White-throated Kingfisher high in the trees, it was a moment of sheer delight. Everywhere I stepped, new birds seemed to pop out of the trees and bushes to greet me: here, another blackbird, there a Cetti's Warbler, and there a Graceful Prinia. I walked the same path I had taken the evening before, back down to the waters of the lake. I wasn't going to miss a chance to see the sun rise over the Gadaran hills, spilling orange beauty over the Sea of Galilee. As I stood there, counting birds and drinking in the majesty of the mountains around me, I could not help but overflow with gratitude. The bright disc of the sun began to slide up over the rim of the world, turning the water gold. Once again, I had the pleasure of watching that quiet, awestruck moment of dawn, when, just for the briefest of times, everything is revealed in an almost unspeakable beauty of both softness and grandeur.

And then, the greatest stroke of all: I looked up to see a flock of very large birds approaching, flying over the rim of the lake. As they flapped their way straight overhead, there was no mistaking the weirdly graceful shapes and startling colors of Greater Flamingos. This, another new species for me, was one of my most exhilarating finds in Israel. Fully satisfied, I turned back toward the hotel, drinking in the awe-inspiring shape of Mount Arbel as it glowed in the morning light.

There was no single, particular moment there on the Sea of Galilee that stuck with me in transformative power. Nevertheless, there was a kind of inexplicable peace in that place that must have worked down into my soul during my days there, because it was that place, the shore of the Sea of Galilee, that retained an almost mystical quality in my memories for months thereafter. The hills and the sea pulled at my heart with a wild and wonderful gravity, even from half a world away. I felt, strangely enough, that I had met a part of Jesus there by the lake, a part of him that I hadn't really known deeply before; and now, when I picture the Savior in my mind's eye, it's almost always there that I see him: there in that place between the water and the setting sun and the dramatic rim of hills around, where he and I shared the same wonder, two thousand years apart. I felt as if I had found a resting-place for my soul, one that was always available to me, in the intertwining beauty of Christ and Galilee.

THE SCENE OF OUR
LORD'S SIGNS

We shall come to the Sea of Gennesaret, where the
five thousand were filled with five loaves... Our eyes
will also look on Capernaum, the scene of so many
of our Lord's signs—yes, and on all Galilee besides.
And when, accompanied by Christ, we shall have
made our way back ... then we shall sing heartily, we
shall weep copiously, we shall pray unceasingly....
We shall say to one another: 'I have found Him
whom my soul loveth; I will hold Him and will not
let Him go.'

—Jerome, *Letter 46*

During the few short years of his ministry in Galilee, Jesus
adopted the town of Capernaum as his home base. There he
lodged, where some of the disciples lived, and there he did many

of his miracles of healing and restoration. Jesus is so closely associated with the town that its ruins today are marked with a large sign at the entry, declaring simply, "the Town of Jesus." Here, as we might have expected, the place was bustling with pilgrims. In the twenty-first century as well as the first, the name of Jesus brought throngs of people to the little town.

Jesus appears to have had an interesting relationship with his adopted hometown. He could frustrate local leaders and entrance the crowds at the same time. Those in authority didn't always know what to do with Jesus, but they were willing to turn to him in moments of need. Jesus, for his part, showed both a restlessness and his rootedness. He would leave the town regularly, telling his disciples that he had a responsibility to preach the Kingdom in other towns, too—but he would always come back, at one time or another, to Capernaum.

———·———

I suspect that my pilgrimage with God has a lot more to do with the idea of "home" than I would have previously guessed. It's something I'm still discovering about myself. I was a child of missionaries, and my growing-up years were split between Brazil, a missionary training camp in Texas, and our family's home area in Maine. It was an upbringing that I would not have traded for anything else in the world, and still would not today. But where, if anywhere, did I actually belong? I recall thinking of Maine as "home," even when I had scarcely spent any of my life there. I can remember arriving back in Maine from Brazil at the end of one trip, and fondly spelling out the letters of the state's name in my mind, as if telling myself that this was where I belonged. But as I look back on it now, that was a little strange, seeing that the only home of which I had any actual memories was a continent away.

But this sort of longing for home—and a perpetual uncertainty about whether one actually belongs there, or somewhere else—is not unusual for someone with my background. One of the professors at my college, David Pollock, helped establish a new field in intercultural studies and psychology, dealing with the experience of TCKs (third-culture kids): children raised abroad by expatriate parents. A common feature of this group, including me, is the sense that they don't completely belong either to the surrounding culture in which they grew up, nor to their parents' home culture (thus, they have their own "third" culture). I never thought much about this as a kid, but as I look back over my life now, it comes out strongly. Though I can adapt to innumerable conditions, can thrive in a broad array of circumstances, I still labor against a sense, in lots of the places where I go, that I never quite belong. This tendency even shows up in my writing: I've written nine novels, and not one of them is set in the main character's home area. They all involve some kind of quest or journey, and in many cases, my characters are either longing for a lost home, or they have a conflicted narrative about the homes they've left behind.

Why does this matter? Because I can see the same kind of struggle with "home" in my spiritual walk. My walk with God has always been a pilgrimage on which I have yearned forward with desperate intensity, always trying to move to a new stage, never content with where I actually was. For me, it was an experience of seeking that "untraveled world, whose margin fades for ever and for ever when I move," in the words of Tennyson's old poem. I am constantly longing to move toward my spiritual homeland—a purified, restful, contented union with the holiness of God—but those yearnings sometimes leave me discontented with the vales I must walk to get there. And all this, I suspect, may have something to do with the shape of my early years, and my unstated but persistent desire to belong somewhere.

We often carry the shape of our journeys into our walk with God. My story has geared me toward always longing to go "further up and further in" (to use C. S. Lewis's turn of phrase). And that's sometimes an asset, and sometimes a hindrance. But that's the way of all life, isn't it? We bear with us our own distinctive ways of thinking and acting, and those patterns mold our assumptions and desires regarding everything we do, including the Christian life.

But the marvelous thing about God is that he meets us where we are. Jesus, when he encounters his disciples on the shorelines of Capernaum, accepts them in their current state of life, and he values them for their distinctive differences. His nicknames for his closest friends, "Rock" (Peter), and "Sons of Thunder" (James and John), reveal a deep fondness for their personalities. So however your journey has shaped you—whether it's toward yearning and striving, like me, or toward peaceful rest in the arms of a loving Father—know that Jesus meets you precisely in those things, and loves you as you are.

———·———

Capernaum is no longer a living city, but the remains of the first-century town lie open to the gaze. The shoreline has receded from where the town now sits, but you can still see the waves of the lake behind a field of grass, where a beautiful, red-domed Orthodox church now sits to commemorate the site. As for the town itself, only the bases of the stone walls remain: the footings and passages where houses—extraordinarily small houses—used to stand. All of the stones were dark, almost black, and Norah explained that the first-century village had been built out of local basalt, a dark volcanic rock. It's one of those little details that never makes it into movies or shows about the life of Jesus, so a tour of the real Capernaum still carries some surprises for the modern visitor.

To the right of this field of walls was a large, disc-like modern building, an octagonal church that had been built up on pillars to hover over a portion of the ruins. And on the left was an equally impressive edifice, though far older: the synagogue of Capernaum, with many walls and pillars still standing. Around the edge of the yard were a row of displays from the capitals and friezes of the synagogue, including one that showed an ancient use of the Star of David. Norah told us that the six-pointed star was a long-standing symbol of the faith of Israel, and one theory of its meaning was that it represented the downward-stretching arms of God crossing with the upward-stretching arms of humanity, as if reaching to embrace one another.

It was to the synagogue we first directed our attention. Though the standing walls and pillars were made of white stone, and represented a later, third or fourth-century construction, it had been built directly atop the first-century synagogue, and the black basalt foundation could still be plainly seen. Its size was impressive for a town that small—an indication that the Gospels' account of wealthy benefaction was exactly right. We slipped into the synagogue and sat down on the stone benches in the back corner. It had no roof anymore, so the whole building was washed in brilliant sunlight, and the white pillars seemed to shine. We called to mind the scenes that had played out there: the dramatic works that Christ had done in that synagogue, healing the demon-possessed, the sick, and the injured.

As impressive as the synagogue was, though, it was the site at the other end of Capernaum that fascinated me the most. It was also, clearly, the main attraction for most other pilgrims: in the little area under the edge of the hovering modern church, just where one could peer in to see what lay underneath, was a sea of people, all packed in tight and craning their necks to catch a glimpse of the ruins beyond. While a bit of a nuisance, this struck me as perfectly appropriate. Why? Because under that church lay the remains of a house that had been reverenced by Christians going all the way back to the first century itself. According to tradition (and backed up by substantial archaeological evidence), this was the house belonging to Peter and his family, where Jesus healed Peter's mother-in-law, and where Jesus himself may have taken up residence for a while. It was also sometimes identified as the very house where a vast crowd of people had thronged in to hear him, a mass of people so impenetrable that the paralytic's four friends had to cut a hole in the roof to get to Jesus.

Now we had the honor of sharing the same experience: trying to shoulder our way into the densely-packed crowd so that we could see the remaining walls of the house. We did our little mini-service before plunging in, and then we found a gap in the crowd and were able to work our way up to the railing. I was glad for the chance to be there, looking at the stones of the very house where Jesus carried out his ministry, still here after two thousand years. Yet I felt no deep spiritual impression from being there. My hopes, as always in my pilgrimage, lay somewhere up ahead.

THE GARDEN OF BEATITUDE

And lo! I find a healing balm,
The world grows dim to me;
My spirit rests in sudden calm
With Him of Galilee.

—Henry Warburton Hawkes,
"Amid the Din of Earthly Strife"

One of the regular features of Jesus' work was his preaching, and Matthew records a major section of his teachings in the Sermon on the Mount (Luke, for his part, also records a similar sermon). This sermon, encompassing three whole chapters (Matt. 5-7), is set "on a mountainside" (5:1), while Luke has his parallel account happening "on a level place" (Lk. 6:17). Now, it's possible that the Gospels record two separate sermons, since it seems likely that Jesus would have presented his teachings in multiple locations. But it just so happens that there is a spot along the north-west shore of the Sea of Galilee, not far from Capernaum, that could be described both as "on a mountainside" and "on a level place." The traditional site for this sermon sits upon a mountain slope that rises from the waters, but in a place where the incline is so gentle as to be nearly flat.

The opening section of Matthew's version of the sermon includes the famous list of Beatitudes, so the location has come to be called "the Mount of Beatitudes." Many thousands of books have been written on Jesus' teachings in the Sermon on the Mount, which continue to challenge hearers two thousand years later. Jesus' words are confident, even forceful, and insist on a real, lived-out Christian morality that aims to emulate the perfect holiness of God. These words have inspired whole movements, all through the history of the church, from the Anabaptists' insistence on practical holiness to Martin Luther King, Jr.'s ethic of nonviolent resistance.

These three chapters have also changed my life in a very direct and pro-found way. When I was a teenager, my brother Josh and I attempted to memo-rize large chunks of Scripture together. Memorization of individual verses was a regular part of our upbringing in Sunday School and youth group, but we had never attempted to memorize whole chapters at a time. So we took on Matthew 5–7 as one of our first challenges, the Sermon on the Mount, and over the course of a few weeks, we had committed the entirety of it to memory.

And little by little, I started to notice some changes. I had something of a temper when I was a teen, especially towards my family, and it came out every now and then in outbursts of rage. But during that season where I was committing Jesus' words to memory, my anger just seemed to go away. It van-ished like mist under the gentle pressure of Jesus' teaching, and it has never been a problem for me since that day. I can claim no credit for that—it wasn't because of my willpower or spiritual maturity, as my ongoing struggles with other sins gave ample evidence over the years—so it must have been a work of grace through the power of the Word of God. There's something about mem-orization that brings the voice of Scripture down into the deepest recesses of one's mind and soul, far deeper than willpower alone can go, and it can do wonders there. Jesus' admonitions about loving one's enemies sank down into my bones, and have shaped much of the way I view the world now.

So when I came to the Mount of Beatitudes, I was coming to one of the crucibles of my own formation, a waystation on my pilgrimage where I had supped before. I looked over the church, the garden, and the loveliness of it all with great fondness, for Jesus' words, spoken in that place, had already changed my life.

———·———

This was one of many places in Israel where I wished I could have spent more time. As we got off the bus, faced with a thickly-thronged parking lot, our leaders told us that we would only have a few minutes to look around. We sped through the colonnades of the outer building and into the gardens surrounding the church. We rushed past everything until we found a quiet space in the yard to gather for our quick mini-service. I have to confess that I wasn't all that attentive to our service there; I was caught up in drinking in my surroundings. Whereas most of the surrounding slope was fairly dry and brown, there was a pocket of lush greenery all around the church, a verdant garden that breathed peace into the surrounding air. If we had been there on a less busy day, with a bit more time, it would have been a delightful spot to pause and pray.

I breathed deep of the garden's air as we wrapped up our service. I tried to imagine Jesus there on that mountainside, and I thought about the way he began his sermon, with the Beatitudes—the proclamation of those who were blessed, or made happy, in the reality of his Kingdom. The Greek word Jesus uses, *makarioi*, can be translated as either "blessed" or "happy," and you'll find one or the other in any English translation you pick up. In my own poetic rendition of the Beatitudes, I chose to use both: "So happily blessed are the poor …." These words of Jesus have touched many millions of lives, and I was one of those who had been blessed and made happy thanks to the very words that Christ had spoken there.

Once again, it was the birds of the place that cemented this impression in my mind. The garden was full of Rose-ringed Parakeets: common, bright green parrots of medium size, which one can see anywhere in Israel, they cut through the air with swift beauty, trailing long, elegant tails, and amid their emerald plumage you can sometimes see a flash of red around their necks. And as with most parrots, they just seem happy. It makes one smile to see them. I had seen a few here and there already in Israel, but never as many as in that garden around the Church of the Beatitudes. They clustered in the tree beside our mini-service; they poked their curious heads out of the crevices in the trunks of giant palm trees; they even sat in reverent bliss on the church's metal cross. Their happy presence seemed to me a fitting thing for the place where Jesus proclaimed the blessedness of living in his Kingdom. Now, when-ever I think of the Beatitudes, I picture the arcing, beautiful flight of emerald parakeets in the trees of the garden.

I made a quick circuit through the church's interior before we left. It was small, as were many of the pilgrim chapels in Israel, only accommodating space for about twenty worshipers at a time. But it was lovely: bright sun-light spilled in through the cupola of the dome, where each of the Beatitudes was written in Latin. In the center of the octagonal space stood an altar-table, and around it a circular aisle where one could make the circuit of the church. Again it struck me as a marvelous place to pray, if only we had been there on a calmer day with more time to spare. But such are the drawbacks of only hav-ing eight days in Israel.

THE BREAD OF LIFE

Break Thou the bread of life, dear Lord, to me,
As Thou didst break the loaves beside the sea.
Beyond the sacred page I seek Thee, Lord;
My spirit pants for Thee, O Living Word.

—Mary Lathbury, "Break Thou the Bread of Life"

Our next stop was just a short way down the hillside, close to the shoreline of the Sea of Galilee. The name of the place was Tabgha, and it had long been regarded as the traditional site for the feeding of the five thousand. All four Gospels have stories about Jesus' miraculous feedings, so it was an experience that must have stuck in the disciples' minds. The Christian tradition has always placed value not only on fasting, but also on feasting, and this miracle was a feast indeed: a celebration of the gracious providence of God, whose blessings meet and exceed our every need. While fasting can help to rein in and tame the desires of the body, feasting takes a different tack, and turns those desires toward their proper purpose by using them to delight in God's goodness and render our thanks to him.

We don't often think about eating as a spiritual act, but it is. Eating is part of our relationship with God. It's no accident that the most precious ritual of our faith is a ritual of eating, nor that the Bible's creation accounts are so insistent on the centrality of food to humanity's existence (Gen. 1:29; 2:9, 16–17), including, of course, the fact that the first sin involved an act of eating. Much of Jesus' ministry happens around dinner-tables, where he eats with sinners, tax collectors, and, occasionally, even with Pharisees. Early Christian worship probably involved not only a ritual of communion, but a shared meal as well (Acts 2:46; 1 Cor. 11:33; Jude 12).

The Orthodox theologian Alexander Schmemann, in his book *For the Life of the World,* notes that we were designed, from the very beginning, as eating beings, and that this reflects our role as God's priests. Throughout the Old Testament, one of the main responsibilities of priests was eating, whether the daily Bread of the Presence, or the meat that was presented as part of people's sacrifices.

We, too, were created to be priests of God (a vocation returned to us in Christ—1 Pet. 2:5, 9; Rev. 1:6; 5:10), and by eating, we accept the offerings of creation as the blessings of God, and use it to render thanks and praise to him. Every time we eat, we are essentially taking something that God has given, and making it part of ourselves: thus building our lives—in the most literal possible sense—upon the blessings of God. This is why it's such a fitting thing to give thanks to our Creator for what he has provided every time we eat—it's not just a legalistic rule that you have to say grace before a meal; it shows a properly-ordered sense that eating is meant to be an act of worship.

Eating, then, is part of our relationship with God—and not just eating at communion or church potlucks, but all of our eating. Our society runs desperately after every new fad diet to try to regulate its out-of-balance relationship with food. But the only way to regain our balance is to remember that we were created as holistic beings, bodies and souls together, so eating can never be simply a bodily act. God must be a part of our eating. Food is not an end in itself, and even the healthiest dieting gurus misuse food by their attention on the body alone. The spiritual discipline of feasting is not just for the purpose of enjoying flavors, filling our bellies, or calming our rattled nerves, not even just for promoting good health: it is meant to direct our joy and gratitude to God.

So when Jesus miraculously multiplies the loaves and fishes, he is welcoming the people to receive from his hand, as from the divine Giver of all good things. Just like God fed his people manna and quail in the wilderness, so Jesus feeds his people bread and fish in a remote place by the lake. Jesus begins by giving thanks to God the Father (Luke 9:16), thus inviting them to make their eating a part of their worship. And then he gives them all that they need, and more besides. When we are receiving our blessings from the hand of Christ, we always have all that we need, whether in plenty or in want.

———·———

The traditions pointing to Tabgha as the site of the feeding of the five thousand go all the way back to the early days of Byzantine Christianity, and perhaps before. In fact, one of the marks of Tabgha's fame is precisely that ancient pedigree. It was there, in the ruins of a Byzantine church marking the spot, that one of the truly iconic pieces of Christian artwork was discovered: a mosaic, beautiful in its simplicity, showing a bowl with four loaves, flanked by two fish. Notice that while the Gospel story includes five loaves in the feeding of the five thousand, the mosaic only shows four. Why? Because Jesus himself is the bread of life, and in that spot, above where the mosaic lies at the altar, the fifth loaf—the symbol of Christ's own body—is still being broken and shared among the people. The mosaic shows the loaves after one has been removed, and this is intended to remind us that we, in celebrating the communion of our Lord, are participating in his great act of provisioning us with his infinite life.

I've always loved the story of the feeding, because it spoke to me on a personal level. It was a keen reminder of the fact that no matter how small and frail were the gifts and talents that I could offer up to God, he could still take them and do something incredible. So although the little boy at Tabgha had nothing more than a simple lunch with him, it was enough in Jesus' hands to feed the multitudes. And although I had only a few small things to offer, even those things could be made effective for the Kingdom in the hands of the Lord.

The little church of Tabgha—slightly larger than that of the Beatitudes, but with far fewer pilgrims—was one of the most peaceful places I have ever been. It was simple, but gorgeous and breathtaking and restful, all at once. The part of the church I really loved, though, was a partially restored mosaic in the corner of the sanctuary: a vast, intricate, artful display of many different kinds of birds. The mosaic, hailing from more than a millennium and a half ago, was so detailed that I could still identify many of the different species portrayed there. It was a charming reminder that I, in my ornithological obsessions, was not as much of an oddity as one might have thought. I was not the first pilgrim to have been captivated by the loveliness of Israel's birds.

FINDING SHELTER
IN HIS GLORY

God is so good, He wears a fold
Of heaven and earth across His face—
Like secrets kept, for love untold.
But still I feel that His embrace
Slides down by thrills through all things made,
Through sight and sound of every place:
As if my tender mother laid
On my shut lids her kisses' pressure,
Half waking me at night; and said,
"Who kissed you through the dark, dear guesser?"

—Elizabeth Barrett Browning, "A Child's Thought of God"

Mount Tabor is the traditional site for the story of the Transfiguration, where Jesus' glory is revealed before his disciples' wondering eyes. No one is really sure where this story might have happened; the Gospels simply don't give us enough historical detail to answer the question with any measure of certainty. All we really know is that it was on "a mountain apart," and by that measure, Mount Tabor is one of several sites that fits the bill. It is indeed a mountain apart, rising in singular majesty from the plains below, and a mountain that would have been well-known to Jesus, standing in relative proximity to both Nazareth and the Sea of Galilee.

Popular nineteenth-century pilgrims' accounts tell harrowing stories of ascending Mount Tabor—tales of weariness, cantankerous pack animals, and the constant danger of getting lost on the slopes. The experience today is a good deal smoother and quicker, but still a little harrowing. Because of the steepness of the slopes, the road up to the peak, full of hairpin switchbacks, is not open to tour buses. Instead, pilgrims are asked to park at the base of the slope and get a ride in one of several tightly-packed vans operated by local drivers. I was wedged into the front-row passenger seat along with another pilgrim, and I got a marvelous view straight down the many cliff faces of Mount Tabor whenever we careened around a switchback turn. Had I ever suffered from a fear of heights, it might have been a terrifying journey, but I've had my fair share of eye-opening traffic experiences from all around the world, and I found that I rather enjoyed it.

Here, as in many places along our tour of Israel, memories of the Crusades are everywhere. The pilgrimage-sites of Israel are a snapshot of the whole world of Christianity: while most of the local traditions represent the Orthodoxy of the East, the Crusades and their legacy left a massive, indelible mark of the Western church on the Holy Land, not only in ruins but in active religious communities that have existed there from the 1200s until today. So here, on the top of Mount Tabor, Christian East and Christian West met again: an Orthodox church on one side, and a Roman Catholic on the other, amid the tumbledown ruins of Crusader walls. And in and amongst all the pathways walked a hundred pilgrims from every nation and denomination upon the earth.

Bright sunshine washed over us, and golden flowers displayed their glories on every side. Even the birds seemed attracted by the radiance of the place: a Palestine Sunbird flashed its emerald plumage along the slope; a Sardinian

Warbler flitted through the tops of cypress trees along the way, and Alpine Swifts cut sweeping arcs through the blue sky all around.

As was our practice, before we walked around or viewed the church, we found a wayside spot to gather and do a little service. As it happened, the church was surrounded by the ruins of an old Benedictine monastery, and it was the little chapel of that community that hosted our gathering. Here I told the second of the stories that had been assigned to me: like the Annunciation, I had chosen the story of the Transfiguration because it meant something to me. During an earlier stage of my spiritual journey, it had been Orthodox theology that helped bring me out of a season of doubt, and ancient Orthodox reflections made much of the Transfiguration. Naturally, I didn't seize the moment to launch into a treatise on early church theology; I merely recited the marvelous story of Christ's transfiguration.

———·——

The Transfiguration story is sometimes misunderstood. We, who trust too much in our ordinary sense-perceptions, view what happens to Jesus as something wild, strange, out of the ordinary. We regard it, essentially, as something that is *happening* to him, rather than the way he always is. We think the disciples' ordinary, day-to-day perception of Jesus is the accurate one, and so we assume that this display of radiant splendor that surrounds and suffuses the scene is something added from the outside, as if God were shining down a massive spotlight on the mountain for just a moment.

But that's not actually the traditional way to interpret it. Early Christians usually understood this moment to be an "unveiling." It wasn't adding anything to Jesus that he didn't already have, either in his divine or his human nature. Rather, it was that the disciples' eyes were unveiled for a moment to see Jesus as he actually was. There are other stories like this in Scripture. Take, for instance, the opening of Elisha's servant's eyes, to be able to see, for just a moment, the angelic armies that were surrounding and protecting the people of God (2 Kings 6:17). It wasn't that the angels hadn't been there, only to show up at just that moment; it was that he couldn't see them until his eyes were opened. We're in the same position: much of the work of the Kingdom of God goes on behind the scenes, in ways that cannot be captured by news headlines or seen with our physical eyes. The Bible, especially in its apocalyptic books like Daniel and Revelation, reminds us that there are whole dramas going on in the heavens and on the earth which we cannot yet see.

Even modern science tells us that we don't see the world as it actually is: we see a picture that our brain creates for us, translating the wavelengths of light that are bouncing around us into a coherent image. But there are colors that we simply cannot see—real colors, which exist in the actual world, to which we are blind. Other animals can see them, though. So when a hummingbird, which can see ultraviolet wavelengths, looks at a flower, it sees (at least in some sense) a "truer" view of the flower than you and I can ever see. Christianity is not irrational or naïve to believe in an unseen world, nor to insist on walking by faith and not by sight, for, as it turns out, walking by sight alone means that you're not really seeing the whole picture.

Many scholars believe that Jesus, in his ascent up the mount of transfiguration, is intentionally evoking the experience of Moses on Mount Sinai. Moses goes up the mountain after a period of six days (Ex. 24:16), and Jesus does the same (Mark 9:2; Matt. 17:1). Moses first approaches the mountain with three others (Aaron, Nadab, and Abihu—Ex. 24:1, 9), and Jesus also chooses three disciples to accompany him (Peter, James, and John). A cloud covers Mount Sinai while Moses is upon it, and a cloud also covers the mount of transfiguration (Ex. 24:15–16; Mark 9:7). In both cases, the person becomes radiant—in Moses' case, so radiant that he has to wear a veil over his face when interacting with other Israelites (Ex. 34:29-35). And when the voice of God speaks, identifying Jesus as his beloved Son and exhorting the disciples to "listen to him," this is a direct fulfillment of the promise of a prophet like Moses, of whom the Israelites were told, "listen to him" (Deut. 18:15). Peter's remark after the event, that they should build shelters for everyone on the mountaintop, is essentially a recognition of this connection with the Mount Sinai story. Building shelters was what Jews did every year at the Feast of Tabernacles to honor the presence of glory of God abiding with them, a tradition that went all the way back to the Sinai experience. Though Peter struggles to know the right words to say, his first impulse is to acknowledge the fact that their eyes have been opened to see God's glory.

When the apostle Paul deals with the story of Moses' radiant face in 2 Cor. 3:7–4:6, he suggests that the glory revealed in Christ is not something shining down on Jesus from the outside, but is a glory that is proper to himself. That is to say, the transfiguration wasn't God adding something to Jesus; it was a real, unhindered view of "the glory of Christ, who is the image of God" (2 Cor. 4:4). Jesus Christ was always and forever radiant with glory, but most of the time people couldn't see it, because their minds and hearts were veiled. So although Jesus was mirroring the story of Moses on Mount Sinai when he went to Mount Tabor, it turns out that Jesus was not really standing in the place of Moses in that story: he was standing in place of God himself—the glory of the Lord that looks like a consuming fire (Ex. 24:17).

Further, Paul suggests that we, who now stand in the place of Moses as witnesses to God's glory, are being transformed just as Moses was: "We all, who with unveiled faces contemplate the Lord's glory, are being transformed into his image with ever-increasing glory" (2 Cor. 3:18). That doesn't mean that our faces will literally start to shine, but it does suggest that the change Moses experienced wasn't just some kind of strange, irradiated afterglow. It was the natural consequence of being with the Lord. And we, who draw near to Jesus and contemplate his glory, we too—whether we can see it or not—are being suffused with his glory just as surely as Moses was.

The journey of the Christian, as we follow Jesus and look unto him, is a journey of radical transformation. The transfiguration is not only a story for Jesus and the disciples; it's a story for us, too, and it tells of what wondrous things God does in our frail human nature when we accept his invitation to participate in the glory of his divine nature (2 Pet. 1:4). Though our weak and limited vision cannot always see his hand at work within us, that does not mean that it isn't there.

———————

So we sang and prayed together in our little service, where monks had sung and prayed eight hundred years before, and then began a tour of the church. It was one of the loveliest buildings we saw in the Holy Land: soaring like a cathedral and gilt in golden radiance that called to mind the Gospel story. The interior was uplifting and beautiful, but among its most interesting features were two little side-chapels, one dedicated to Moses and the other to Elijah. So although Peter's suggestion to build shelters wasn't taken up during the time of the Gospels, now you can go to the Mount of Transfiguration and find "shelters" on either side of the church, commemorating both the great lawgiver and the prophet.

At the end of our time on the mountain, I stole a few minutes to wander through the ruins of the old monastery. The peace of that place, and the memory of those old monks, breathed grace to my soul in the midst of a day where it felt like we were always on the run. At the end of my explorations,

I happened upon a chapel where I found one of the loveliest Orthodox icons I had ever seen—a cruciform painting of Jesus at his death. It felt as if it had been left there to minister to my heart: that I, who had gained so much inspiration from the early-church roots of the Orthodox faith, should find such a beautiful symbol of that very same tradition waiting for me at the end of my walk through the monastery. It was a reminder to me that this place—and all the places of the Gospels—were the scenes of Jesus' signs, laid out not only for his own disciples to see, but for all his followers throughout history. The story of the transfiguration was my story, the story of Jesus' glory radiating in my life, and it felt like I had received a personal welcome there on Mount Tabor: a shelter not only for Moses and Elijah, but for me.

THE DAY OF DESOLATIONS

Make my mortal dreams come true
With the work I fain would do;
Clothe with life the weak intent,
Let me be the thing I meant . . .

—John Greenleaf Whittier, "Andrew Rykman's Prayer"

Jesus' work around Galilee was not limited to feeding multitudes and doling out pithy beatitudes. He also had to do quite a lot of rebuking, challenging, warning, and even calling down a few prophetic woes. There were lots of people around the Sea of Galilee that didn't want Jesus around. He was perpetually confronted by religious leaders who were offended by his teachings; he was cast off by the rich and powerful, whom he made uncomfortable with his clear-sighted morality; and every now and then he was forced to leave a place of rejection and move on to another spot.

One of our days of touring in Galilee lined up a few different spots of curses, rebukes, and expulsions. In addition to Dan (an Old Testament site featuring an illegitimate cult center), we stopped at Caesarea Philippi, a pagan temple complex where Jesus had referenced "the gates of hell," at Chorazim, over which he declared prophetic woes, and then also at Kursi, where he was expelled from the region after healing the man afflicted by a legion of demons.

Our first order of business that day was to drive a bit north and east of the lake, toward the Syrian border, where we visited the ruins of the ancient city of Dan. The only story that stuck in my memory about Dan was one of infamy: that the early rulers of the divided kingdom had set up a rival worship site there, in opposition to Jerusalem's Temple. In fact, a portion of that site survives: the location of the massive altar and the high place where Jeroboam and others authorized unlawful sacrifices.

The major point of interest for me was not the city of Dan itself, but the remnants of a much more ancient structure: a gateway arch that had stood in that spot since the days of Abraham, and which the patriarch himself might well have seen on his journey into Canaan. I paused to pray that Abraham's courageous obedience might be given, at least in some small way, to my own uncourageous and disobedient heart. It was there that I first glimpsed the great, slowly-circling funnels of White Storks reaching high up into the sky— like Abraham, on his journey from Ur to Canaan, these storks made the long, soaring trek from Africa to Europe every year.

Nearby the old city of Dan was a site from the Gospels: the Herodian resort-town of Caesarea Philippi. Here one of the headwaters of the Jordan River emerges near a cliff that once housed a massive shrine to the pagan god Pan. The broad cave of the sacred grotto is still there, a gaping maw in the center of the cliff. In Jesus' day, it stood alongside a temple to the Roman emperor and several smaller shrines. Interestingly, it was in this very spot—this very unlikely, very pagan spot—that Jesus chose to ask his disciples about his identity. And here, in the shadow of temples built to worldly empires and false gods, Simon Peter proclaimed the truth of the gospel: "You are the Christ, the Son of the living God!" The location of this story adds to its meaning: Jesus' identity is set against the claims of the false gods and the pagan emperor, and it triumphs over them. It wasn't uncommon for Roman emperors to claim titles like "son of god" or "savior," but the Gospels insist in no uncertain terms that Jesus alone is heir to such magnificent titles.

Jesus, perhaps standing in sight of the great rock face of the cliff, commends Simon, names him Peter, and says "On this rock I will build my church, and the gates of hell shall not prevail against it!" As it happens, there's an old tradition that the pagan shrine at Caesarea Philippi was believed to be an opening to the underworld—quite literally, the gates of hell. And standing there two millennia later, I could see the truth of Christ's prophecy with my own eyes: the shrines of Pan and the pagan gods were dust, and the church of Jesus Christ was standing strong all across the world. (As we left the cliff at Caesarea Philippi, I noted with ironic pleasure that there was a native species of bird that called "the gates of hell" its home: the Rock Pigeon, or as we call it, the common city pigeon. That's somehow fitting, as I'm sure you'll agree.)

———·———

You might say that that day in Galilee was our "day of desolation," our tour of the sites of tragedies and judgments. By a strange turn of fortune, it was also a day of spiritual desolation for me—or at least a humbling reminder of my own weakness. After we left Caesarea Philippi, I faced three temptations in quick succession. If I can dare to suggest such a thing, it almost hearkened back to Satan's three temptations of Christ in the desert, such was the sense that it was being planned out against me. In my case, however, unlike Christ, I managed to avoid the temptations in stumbles and half-measures, rather than by triumphant recitations of Scripture. The other main difference between Christ and myself, as you'll see, is that whereas Satan aimed his temptations at Jesus toward levels only reserved for divine figures ("Come on, do a miracle! You know you want to!"), mine appeared geared toward the lowest common denominator of base human instinct, to the extent that they may strike the reader as almost trivial.

First, an opportunity came along, after a long morning of walking in the hot sun, to indulge in some good old-fashioned American gluttony. We stopped at that most authentic purveyor of global cuisine, a McDonald's. Yet in that moment, while I might have wanted to order a double set of supersized meals and scarf it all down at once, I contented myself with a normal lunch (at least by McDonald's standards). Second, just beyond the balcony of the restaurant, down in a gully, was one of the clear-rushing upper currents of the Jordan, and while my fellow tour-mates were still getting their food, I noticed that there was a young woman down there in a vanishingly small swimsuit. With her down there, and me high up on the balcony overhead, it felt staged to be a Bathsheba moment. Thankfully, unlike King David, I managed to refrain from seducing her and killing off her spouse, and instead went back to my lunch. Then, as we drove away, a third temptation: a comment from my brother Josh, who, as older brothers are wont to do, felt the need to correct and clarify an observation of mine, which made me feel all the natural resentment and wounded pride of a younger sibling. But I'm not clever enough to come up with withering retorts on the spot, so I didn't bother responding, and just settled back into my seat to wait for our next stop.

Obvious offers toward gluttony, lust, and pride: the tempter must not have had a very high opinion of my defenses. But, truth be told, even though none of these little darts really hit the mark with me that day, I still felt the sting of them. True, my outward behavior did not sway, and I didn't waver from doing what I thought was right. But temptations like these still remind me that the barbs of my sinful disposition remain lodged somewhere deep. Rather like the pull of a magnet, I can feel something within me ready to respond to temptation when it draws near. In this case, while I didn't waver, I still felt that magnetic pull, and the fact that I said no to it every time probably has more to do with the company I was keeping, and the public nature of any willful sin in the middle of a pilgrimage group, than to any great strength on my part. As Mark Twain once said, "There are several good protections against temptation, but the surest is cowardice." So I'm not sure I can count all those moments to my credit.

The rapid-fire sequence of these temptations, and my awareness that it was inconvenience and timidity, rather than full-fired holiness, that kept me from following them, added up to a small dose of discouragement. There I was in the Holy Land, yearning to become possessed of a thoroughgoing purity of life, thought, and practice, and yet my heart could still be tugged away by even the simplest temptations. Now, I realize that this may sound like a very silly story: aren't I making too much of three surpassingly common experiences, none of which amounted to anything? Probably so, but I tell them because the experiences to follow would reverse all three in an interesting way. It wasn't only the tempter who had staged a bit of moral theater for me that day.

The sites of Chorazim and Kursi were interesting, but offered me no consolation. It was sobering to stand amid the ruins of a town that heard Jesus' words of judgment after their rejection of God's call. And at Kursi, as we looked over the cliffs where, two thousand years ago, Jesus delivered the demoniac and sent his tormentors off amid the swine, I looked in vain for anything that could carry off my own vices from me. But there was only me on the cliff, and the spirit of Christ all around me. I knew that he could deliver me, just as he had for the demoniac so many years ago; and I knew that I, if empowered by his grace, could learn to walk in obedience. But it was a slower road, and a harder one, than I had hoped and imagined it might be.

The old saints often said that the closer we grew to Christ, the greater our awareness of our sins would be. That realization, as I was coming to experience it in my own life, was a difficult one: though I had grown into victory and obedience over many sins in my life as a disciple, I was finding that there were always still more to fight: not only old temptations, but new visions of the depth to which sinful nature had sunk its darksome roots into the human heart. As the Holy Spirit does his work in our hearts, we begin to see sins that we didn't even know were there—attitudes and patterns of the heart and mind that run beneath the surface, which try to turn us ever more toward ourselves rather than toward God. Most perniciously of all, these deep-running attitudes can even masquerade as good and noble deeds. Sometimes even a deeply Christian desire—say, a yearning for holiness—might have more to do with a self-focused discontentment than with a God-oriented longing.

There's a story from the days of the desert fathers, having to do with Moses the Black, a violent brigand who came to faith and embarked on the life of a monastic hermit. Early on in his new life, he was having difficulty overcoming his habitual patterns of sin, like the anger that burned inside him, and he became tremendously frustrated with himself. Abba Isidore, Moses' mentor, took him up to a rooftop one night to watch, to pray, and to wait for the sunrise. And as they watched, hour upon hour, they began to see the slow glimmer of light return to the sky—so slow that its progress was almost imperceptible. Little by little, the heavens went from black to darkest blue, then a touch of gray, then slowly a pinkness that heralded the orange light of dawn. And then, finally, the sun rose. Though it had taken hours of waiting, there was no denying that the night was gone and the day had come. And then Isidore reminded his pupil that the work of God's grace in the human heart was like the rising of the sun—wildly transformative, yes, but calling for a patience that endured through all the long moments when the sky was still gray.

———·———

As afternoon drifted slowly toward evening on our day of desolations, we stopped at Yardenit, where the Jordan River exits from the southern end of the Sea of Galilee. The riverbank there, clothed in verdant tranquility, has been arranged to give access to Christian pilgrims who want to experience baptism in the waters of the Jordan, just as Christ did. While this is not the likeliest historical location for Jesus' baptism (that would be the one further south, near Jericho), it is the loveliest. All along the walls of the site, the Gospel story is written in dozens of different languages. As we walked along, I watched other pilgrims, caught up in the joy of walking with their Lord, waiting to be baptized. Right next to the stairs that would lead us down to the water was another group of Christians, where several young women, clad in the purity of white robes and radiant smiles, were awaiting their turn.

Though all of those in our pilgrimage group had already been baptized, Josh provided the opportunity to be immersed in the waters of the Jordan as a reminder of those baptisms, and as a means of sharing more closely the experience of Jesus. Several of our ladies went down to get immersed, and then I and a few others opted for a simpler rite of being anointed with the Jordan's waters in the sign of the cross. So I stood there in humility before my pastor-brother, against whom, earlier that same day, my wounded pride had silently flared. He stooped and drew water up in his cupped hand, spoke to remind me that I was a beloved child of God, and anointed my forehead with the waters of Christ's own baptism.

Here once again was yet another reminder of the grace that overcomes our sins with irresistible power. I suddenly became aware that my three earlier temptations had each been flipped on its head in that very moment. I had faced the triple pull of gluttony, lust, and pride, and now, just a few hours later, I stood face to face with Christ's offer of grace over all three. In place of gluttony, I now stood hungry (it was suppertime, and I had taken no food all afternoon), and yet in the midst of this experience of sharing Christ's journey, I had not even given my hunger a thought. In place of lust, where I had previously looked down and seen a beautiful woman swimming in the waters of the upper Jordan, now I looked down on that same river and saw my sisters in Christ, clothed in white and robed in joy. And in place of pride, where I had resented my brother's pedantic corrections, now I delighted in receiving grace from his hand. Just as Jesus had given Peter three chances to reaffirm his love for Christ on the heels of his three denials, so now he poured out triple graces over my bumbling, half-hearted attempts to follow his ways. In the midst of our dry spells and desolations, the living water of the grace of Christ is still coursing through our lives, ready to cleanse and to restore if we would only come and receive.

SUNDAY MORNING JOY

Give me my scallop-shell of quiet,
My staff of faith to walk upon ...
My gown of glory, hope's true gauge,
And thus I'll take my pilgrimage ...
Then the holy paths we'll travel,
Strewed with rubies thick as gravel ...
No cause deferred, nor vain spent journey,
For there Christ is the King's attorney ...
When the grand twelve-million jury
Of our sins with dreadful fury
'Gainst our souls black verdicts give,
Christ pleads his death, and then we live.

—Sir Walter Raleigh, "The Passionate Man's Pilgrimage"

As dawn broke on our last day in Galilee, I was out again among the birds, listening to the soft splendor of the morning air caressing the rushes of the marsh. We were soon headed south: after breakfast, we were going down from Galilee, along the old Jordan Valley road toward Jericho, and then finally up the hills to Jerusalem. In that one day, we would be undertaking the very pilgrimage that Christ himself took before his passion. With his Galilean ministry complete, Jesus was going up to Jerusalem for the Passover.

But there was an ache in my heart. It was Sunday, and I was wishing I had pressed harder in the planning stages of our pilgrimage to see if I could find a way to get to a church service. But I hadn't done so, and it wasn't on our itinerary. So I reconciled myself to that reality, and boarded the bus with my tour-mates. We might not get the sort of proper church service I wanted, but we would be able to continue to enjoy the fellowship of one another's company, the joy of incarnating Gospel stories to one another in our mini-service recitations, and the pleasure of singing the praises of God in the Holy Land. And that was no small thing. We drove south through Tiberias and then down toward the Jordan road, and I caught my final glimpse of the Sea of Galilee.

Our first stop of the day was an ancient city that stood just southwest of the Sea of Galilee, known to the Old Testament Israelites as Beth Shan and to early Christians as Scythopolis. It appears several times in the Bible, in its various incarnations as a Caananite, Philistine, and Israelite stronghold. In Jesus' day it had been re-founded as a Greco-Roman city-state and a member of the league of cities called the Decapolis. Later, Scythopolis would go through several centuries as a Christian city before the Muslim conquest of Palestine and a devastating earthquake brought its period of settlement to a close. Because it contains well-preserved ruins from all of these periods, it is considered a "Disneyland for archaeologists." It was compelling to see the multi-layered historical panorama laid out before us: Greek brothels and Roman bathhouses abutting directly with Christian chapels; pillars of old pagan temples later etched with crosses; and on the ancient tell that rises above the city, the overlapping remains of Egyptian, Canaanite, Philistine, Israelite, Roman, and Byzantine fortifications. (A "tell" is a high mound of archaeological remains, often with multiple levels laid right on top of one another.)

While the vast majority of Jesus' Galilean ministry was done in Jewish towns, the Gospels relate that he crossed into the Decapolis from time to time. And even though only a small portion of his time was spent there, he was apparently well known. The demoniac man that Jesus healed at Kursi went and witnessed in the Decapolis, and the news spread quickly (Mark 5:20). Matthew tells us that large crowds from the Decapolis came out to follow Jesus in his early ministry (Matt. 4:25).

The cities of the Decapolis were organized as Gentile settlements, and life within them was based on pagan civic rites. As such, many pious Jews chose to steer clear of these cities. But Jesus came as the Savior for all people, first for the Jews but not only for the Jews, just as he had proclaimed to his hometown audience in that inaugural sermon in Nazareth. The Greeks and Romans, avoided as they were by godly Jews intent on following the Law, were nonetheless children of God. And God does not abandon his children. Though they had wandered, Jesus would call them back. Even though it was Gentiles who would nail the Messiah to the cross, it was for them, and for all nations, that he bled.

Scythopolis bore witness to this: a city that saw little of Jesus during his ministry would one day, by his outpoured grace, come to tear down its temples and replace them with churches built in his honor. As one looked around Scythopolis, with its pagan columns now etched with crosses, one could almost hear on the wind that great refrain from Handel's *Messiah*, taken from Rev. 11:15: "The kingdom of this world is become the kingdom of our Lord and of his Christ!" That story, which began two thousand years ago, is still pressing on today, and we have the awe-inspiring honor of living, praying, and bearing witness in the age when, at long last, all peoples and nations will be able to hear the message of the Christ who died for them.

———·———

We walked through the old forum of the town, past a pillared colonnade and then up toward the rising hill of the tell. It wasn't hard to see why this place had been so regularly chosen as a site of fortification: the hill commanded a wide view of its surroundings, there at the juncture of the central highlands and the river lowlands, and it was steep enough to give it a formidable advantage in any battle. But there was something even more exciting (at least to me) about the tell: even from a hundred yards away, I could see the sandy banks of its slope and the many holes and burrows there: a perfect spot, I thought, to find one of Israel's most beautiful birds: bee-eaters, clothed like Joseph in a coat of many colors.

About half of our group made the ascent up the tell, and there, amid the ruins of six civilizations, was a flock of gorgeous European Bee-eaters. Now, I'm a history buff, both in my personal interests and in my formal education—and it should tell you something about just how wonderful these birds are that someone like me could stand in one of the most historically fascinating places he's ever been and could only spare a glance or two at the ruins. Most of the time my eyes were pointing at the sky, where I noticed not only the splendors of the bee-eaters in flight, but, circling higher above, a swirling column of migrants. At first I thought it was another group of White Storks on its way up to Europe, but as I looked closer, I saw to my great delight that it was actually a group of Great White Pelicans, making their own pilgrimage over the dry deserts of the West Bank.

There's an old tradition that associates pelicans with the self-sacrificial death of Christ. Folktales in Europe told how a mother pelican would stab her breast with her beak and draw blood to allow her chicks to feed (which is not true, but nesting pelicans do have feeding behaviors which might have been mistaken for this). In any case, pelicans became longstanding symbols of the love of Christ, giving himself up so that others might live. It was another reminder, as we stood in a city that had received and been transformed by the unmerited grace of Christ, that Jesus' love is unbounded, free, and offered to all.

As I had felt so many times since coming to Israel, I had the sense that God was sharing a special delight in sending me something that he knew would thrill me through and through—in this case, that slow-circling column of soaring pelicans. Even if I couldn't join a worship service of a Holy Land church, I could take part in the everlasting round of creation's praise for its Maker. There amid the reminders of the deaths of civilizations, there were also signs of life and beauty on every side: Eurasian Jays calling from the treetops, pomegranate buds blooming from branches, and the rainbow flash of bee-eaters on the hilltop. And there I, an heir of the Gentile world that had turned to Christ, could join my heart in worship with them.

THE JOY OF ALL GENERATIONS

I had expected many things from Jerusalem, but I had not expected this. I had expected to be disappointed with it as a place utterly profaned and fallen below its mission. I had expected to be awed by it; indeed I had expected to be frightened of it, as a place dedicated and even doomed by its mission. But I had never fancied that it would be possible to be fond of it.

—G. K. Chesterton, *The New Jerusalem*

It was finally time, on Sunday in the Holy Land, to see the city that countless ages had exalted in song, "the joy of all generations" (Is. 60:15): Jerusalem, where kings and priests had sung their psalms of praise; Jerusalem, where the divine presence had descended in power on the Temple courts; Jerusalem, where the eternal Son of God had died and rose again, that I might inherit everlasting life.

We drove up the highway from the Jordan Valley, up through the deserts where ancient saints had labored and prayed, until we could finally see the outer fringe of the city's buildings spilling over the hilltops in front of us. These were the towers of the modern city, the eastern suburbs that now stretched far beyond the old city's enclosures, and it gave a running thrill to see them framed against the sky.

Then, with a dreamlike sort of suddenness, we were there. The bus pulled up alongside a curb set high on the Mount of Olives, and out across the narrow valley rose the walls of the Old City, the radiant, golden Dome of the Rock on the Temple Mount, and the steeples of ancient churches beyond. It was a hazy day, but the features and landmarks of the city could be easily seen. In the distance, the blue domes of the Church of the Holy Sepulchre rose in humble splendor from among the buildings behind the Temple Mount. It was the one place in all of Israel that I most longed to see. Our schedule dictated that we wouldn't actually go there until our final day in Jerusalem, but I was already yearning to walk those ancient aisles, to climb the stairs to Golgotha, and to pray in the shadow of the edicule that stands above the empty tomb.

We spent a few minutes in the little curbside park that offered a panoramic view of the Old City, singing a hymn and sharing a prayer together. We were high on the slope of the Mount of Olives, but not all the way to the ridge's crest. There were a few Gospel sites further up—churches dedicated to the Ascension and the teaching of the Lord's Prayer, and further beyond, the tomb of Lazarus—but we were turning our steps the other way, down toward the city.

So we followed the old road down the slope, the route that Christ himself likely would have ridden during his triumphal entry. The road was narrow and quiet, tracing its way alongside the vast cemeteries of faithful Jews, buried on that slope to await their resurrection on the Day of the Lord. It was a steeper incline than I had imagined: steep enough that one almost had to brace with each step. While I knew that donkeys were sure-footed creatures, it gave a slightly different aspect to the Triumphal Entry than the one I had long held: that even amid the shouting and songs of praise, Christ must have been struck by the gravity of the descent that he was making, down, down, down to the valley that lay in the shadow of the Temple's altars.

Some way before we came to the base of the mount, we paused to rest and pray in the little chapel called "Dominus Flevit" (Latin for "the Lord wept"). It commemorates the account in the Gospels where Jesus paused during his entry to Jerusalem, looked out over the city, and lamented its coming woes. The chapel itself is very small—one of the smallest we encountered in the Holy Land—but marvelously designed to evoke the shape of a teardrop. It tapers up to a point at the top, allowing in a beam of light from the heavens, as if to remind us to look upward for hope when we are faced with the darkness and trials of life.

Immediately behind the altar is a broad window that looks out over the Old City of Jerusalem, with the Temple Mount dominating the center. Jesus would have seen that same sight, and would have known (as he predicted) that the beautiful Temple and much of the city would shortly be turned over to total devastation at the hands of Romans (who would sack the city a generation after Jesus' time, in AD 70). On the altar is a colorful seal showing a picture of a mother hen with her chicks, the very image that Christ used when describing his feelings of longing to be able to protect and save the people of Jerusalem from what would befall them. It is a poignant reminder that we serve a God who is not callous or disinterested in the heart-shattering problems of pain, torment, and loss that plague the human experience. Rather, as Jesus showed over and over again in his passion, he is a God who has willingly entered into our pilgrimage of pain, and has carried our journeys of sorrow upon his whip-riven back.

PARALYZED ON THE STEPS TO HEALING

Wherever Jesus appears,
There also is salvation.

—Cyril of Jerusalem, "Homily on the Paralytic by the Pool"

A ccording to the Gospel of John, Jesus had stopped by the pool of Bethesda during one of his earlier visits to Jerusalem. This spring-fed pool was a center of communal life on the northern side of the city, and the properties of its water led many to gather there in hope of a miraculous healing. John tells us that people believed that when an angel stirred the waters, the first person to plunge in would be healed. Jesus meets a paralyzed man on the steps, who has never had the opportunity to receive healing because there is no one to help him down to the water when the opportunity arises, so in his great mercy, Jesus heals the man then and there (John 5:1–9).

When archaeologists in the 1960s confirmed that the deep tanks uncovered a century before were indeed the remains of Bethesda, they were struck by how the description in John exactly fit the reality on the ground. John's details, confirmed at the site, were among the evidence that led atheist historian Robin Lane Fox to concede that John's Gospel, usually suspected by skeptics of being the least historical version of Jesus' story, in fact showed some significant earmarks of historicity.

One of the surprises that pilgrims encounter at the site—at least Protestant pilgrims who are not well-versed in Marian traditions—is that Bethesda lies less than a stone's throw from the traditional site of Mary's birth. As I mentioned in the first Nazareth chapter, "The Place Where It All Began," some ancient Christian traditions hold that Mary spent her young life near the Temple in Jerusalem.

Marking the spot today is the Church of Saint Anne (named for Mary's mother), one of the finest examples of Crusader architecture in the world. It is a beautiful, white-stone cathedral with soaring pillars and arches, remaining essentially as it was eight hundred years ago. Like many churches from the early part of the high middle ages, its walls and pillars were built thick, and the space inside, though tall and soaring, was narrower than in many later cathedrals. But because of the thick stonework of the walls, unbroken by windows, the echoing acoustics of the interior were incredible. So we indulged in a practice that has become common among pilgrims: we sang "Amazing Grace," and listened as the notes washed back around and over us like a rushing angelic flood. We were not a particularly talented group of singers (indicated by the fact that I was always pressed into service as the song leader), but the church clarified and beautified our notes as if we were singing in the inside of a bell.

After a quick visit to the church's crypt, we went back up into the open sunshine and paused to look down into the broad pits, cisterns, and porticos that once formed the pool of Bethesda. The story of the healing that Jesus wrought there had always been one of my favorites, because the question that he asks the lame man seems hauntingly perceptive in its directness and power: "Do you want to be made well?" Many times in my life, when I felt convicted over a sin, that saying would play itself out in the corners of my mind.

As I looked down into the dry depths of the old pool, now strewn with the rubble of ancient stones and patches of green grass, my great, aching longing for holiness welled up inside me again. I wanted to be drinking from the wells of contentment that I imagined would come with knowing that I was living out my identity as one of God's holy ones, sanctified by the work of Christ. Instead, I found myself in that moment just as I had always been: my deepest desires were for God's way, but their translation into consistent practice had gotten muddled somewhere, and I too often found myself weary, lukewarm, and unprayerful. I wanted to be made well. But, like the lame man in the story, I felt paralyzed by an inability to move, by the impossibility of being able to throw myself into the waters of God's healing. I was stuck on the steps, always gazing at the life I wanted, but never able to get there on my own.

Our group found a shady little corner at the far end of the empty pool, and there we held our mini-service. Here, though, there was an addition to our normal pattern: Josh and Scott offered to pray prayers of healing over any of us who wanted one. And so I stepped up before my brother, who knew many of my struggles and had walked my pilgrimage of doubt and faith with me, and he anointed my forehead with oil and prayed for my healing. There was no jaw-dropping miracle there in that moment, at least none that the eyes could see: no lame man getting up and walking about.

But later on, over the weeks and months to come, I eventually came away with the feeling that there was a change that had been wrought—not a full and instantaneous healing, for the deliverance I longed for was the sort that is best crafted over the course of years of lovestruck discipline—but a window was opened for me to see, for the first time, the real possibility of the life I longed for. By the grace of God, I sensed that his hand would be there for me to lean on in the long journey of taking those steps on, one at a time.

A few weeks after my return from Israel, I would hear these words on a prayer podcast, reflecting on the text of 1 John 4:10, and they stuck with me: "In this is love: not that we loved God, but that He loved us and sent His Son. It is God who takes the initiative. All we can do is try to respond. So at times when I feel weary and godless, remember that it is God's saving action, and not my effort, that really counts." I may have felt stuck on the steps to healing, but it is not my frailties or failings that matter in the end. It is God's saving action that really counts, as Jesus takes my hand and lifts me up.

THE WAY THE TEMPLE FACED

Well may the cavern-depths of Earth be shaken, and
    her mountains nod;
Well may the sheeted dead come forth to gaze on a
    suffering God!
Well may the Temple-shrine grow dim, and shadows
    veil the Cherubim,
When he, the chosen one of Heaven, a sacrifice for
    guilt is given!

      —John Greenleaf Whittier, "The Crucifixion"

As we planned our tour of Jerusalem, I was getting nervous. Josh and Norah were shuffling the itinerary around with a fairly free hand. Our original slate of activities for Jerusalem hadn't been cropped of any items, but the order was being shifted, such that the one place that I most wanted to visit in all of Israel—

the Church of the Holy Sepulchre—was looking more and more squeezed in its precarious slot for our final day in the city. The premise behind changing our schedule was a good one: our final two days in Israel marked that nation's Memorial Day, followed by its 70th anniversary of independence, and so we had shifted forward some of our visits that would have otherwise put us in places potentially hostile to Israel and the US on those particular days. But I began to have a nagging feeling that the Church of the Holy Sepulchre might only get a whirlwind tour at best.

———·———

After Jesus enters Jerusalem on Palm Sunday, he goes to the Temple courts. In the synoptic Gospels (Matthew, Mark, and Luke), this is when he cleanses the Temple, driving out the moneychangers, both for their practice of extorting the poor, and for taking over the spaces that had been set aside for Gentile God-fearers to come and worship the Lord. It is a daring act, essentially declaring his authority over the Temple. High priests generally saw to the administration of the Temple, but now the true High Priest steps onto the scene. And it isn't just a priestly act, it is a kingly act as well, following in the footsteps of the Temple reforms of his royal forebears, like King Josiah (2 Kings 23:1–7). It serves as a physical proclamation, at the beginning of Holy Week, that the Messiah has arrived and that he will not be swayed from his purpose. From that point on, all the events of his passion are oriented around those very Temple courts, as if the drama circles a gravitational center in the Holy of Holies itself.

———·———

We ascended toward the Temple Mount from the south, from the direction of David's old city. We could see the ruins of the southern steps where many pilgrims in Jesus' day would have entered the holy precincts. Then the walkway led us up onto the vast open courtyard of the Temple Mount itself, and the sheer scale of it stood as a remarkable testament to the scale of Solomon's achievement (and of Herod's later reconstruction). It was peaceful, almost parklike, with trees and sunshine and a vast fountain in the space between the mosque and the gold-domed shrine. In one wide corner of the platform were arranged remnants of the old Herodian pillars from the first-century Temple, capitals and fragments of the highest workmanship.

I paused for a moment to take in the vast mosque on the southern end—a low, wide building with a series of arched doorways that told the tale of its

Crusader heritage. Like many things on the Temple Mount, it whispered its memories of other faiths. Though now a mosque (and one of the most important mosques in the entire Muslim world), the building on the southern end had begun as a Crusader palace, where Baldwin reigned as king over Jerusalem. It had served as a church, too, and as a headquarters of the Templar Knights, before being turned to its present function. In the same way, the Dome of the Rock itself, the centerpiece of the Temple Mount, had been built as a Muslim shrine, then converted to a church during Crusader rule, before being put back to its original use. It heartened me somewhat to think that I was standing in the midst of old churches, though, truth be told, Christianity didn't have much of a claim to the space: the Muslims were the first post-Jewish rulers to use the Temple Mount as a sacred place, as Byzantine Christians seem not to have given the place a second thought.

You might think, on reading this rambling historical prologue, that I know quite a bit about the history of the Temple Mount. But that's far from the case. I was shocked to discover during this trip that for my whole life, and in the face of clear biblical evidence to the contrary, I had been picturing the Temple Mount entirely backwards. I'm the sort of person who always has maps and pictures in my head, and the map and picture in my head for the Temple always showed the doors pointed west, with the Holy of Holies aligned east, toward the rising sun. This seemed natural to me: old churches were usually aligned this way, and further, it struck me as fitting that the doors would be facing the main parts of the city. As it turns out, however, the Temple was pointed exactly the other way: doors to the east, the Holy of Holies toward the west, and most of the city would have looked up to see the sides or back of the Temple. Its doors were thrown open not toward the city, but toward the promised Messiah who would one day come over the crest of the Mount of Olives.

Well, so I was wrong about its directional orientation. Why does this matter? Let me pick up the narrative of my visit to the Temple Mount to explain. We ascended a short flight of stairs to the upper platform, where the massive, gorgeous shrine of the Dome of the Rock dominated the center of a vast esplanade. Now we were walking close to the hallowed courts of the Temple itself, that scene of so many wonders: of Abraham bringing his son Isaac up Mount Moriah to sacrifice; of David seeing his vision of the Angel of the Lord at Araunah's threshing-floor, where mercy stopped judgment in its tracks; of

Solomon constructing the Temple and the cloud of God's Shekinah-glory filling the place with power; of centuries of priests offering prayers and sacrifices
for the sins of the people; of Jesus teaching and driving out money-changers;
and of the disciples preaching the good news of salvation. All these scenes
whirled through my mind in a moment as I looked up at the gold-plated dome.
I didn't share the same faith that that dome represented, but as a marker for
a place made unspeakably sacred by the great works of God, it was a fittingly
awe-inspiring structure.

But then I started to look around. On one side, just there to the east, was
the Garden of Gethsemane at the base of the Mount of Olives. I thought of
Jesus praying there, and of him looking up to see the Temple before him: the
doors of the entrance and the glowing sacrifice-altar. It was as if he could look
up into the open face of his Father. Then I turned and looked in the other
direction. And there, to the west, were the blue domes of the Church of the
Holy Sepulchre, marking the area of Jesus' crucifixion and burial. And in that
moment it struck me that the position of the Temple really did matter in Jesus'
story. When he was hanging on the cross, dying, he would have been put on
display to face the nearest gate and city wall. And so, facing east, he would have
been looking straight up at the blank back wall of the Temple. When he cried
out, "My God, my God, why have you forsaken me?", the one thing dominating his field of view would have been the Temple, facing away. It was as if God
the Father had, quite literally, turned his back on his Son as the weight of the
world's sin came down on Jesus' shoulders. The Temple faced east, toward the
dawning of a new sunrise, and its back was toward Golgotha.

Suddenly the pain of Jesus' torment on the cross ripped like a floodtide
through my mind. There at the Temple Mount, we weren't just standing in a
place made holy by the Shekinah-presence of God; we were standing at the
axis-point of Christ's own passion. To the east, the Garden of Gethsemane; to
the south, the scene of Jesus' trial at Caiaphas' house; to the north, the Fortress Antonia, the military headquarters of his executioners; and to the west,
the hill of Calvary itself. I was standing in the center of the world, and it was
all about Jesus.

THE CHURCH OF
JESUS' SORROW

Wait on the Lord, ye trembling saints,
And keep your courage up.
He'll raise your spirit when it faints,
And far exceed your hope.

—Isaac Watts, "Soon as I Heard My Father Say" (Ps. 27)

It was the end of our first day in Jerusalem—Sunday, and the afternoon was beginning to fade into a gentle evening. We were standing nearly at the base of the Mount of Olives, with the gully of the Kidron Valley between us and the rising walls of the Temple Mount. And there, cloistered within two walled enclosures on the left and right of the road, lay the quiet paths of Gethsemane. This was where Jesus had gone after sharing his Last Supper with his disciples, a place to pray beneath the shadows of the olive trees while his betrayer went to turn him in.

It's a familiar instinct to me—the need to get away, to find some little patch of forest in which to think, to pray, to breathe. When I studied in London, I used to ride the Tube to Hampstead Heath every now and then, just to find a place where I could quiet my mind away from the frantic pace of city life. Jesus, too, grew up as a country boy, in a little village on a hill in Galilee, and throughout his life he showed a tendency to retreat to the wilderness when he needed to pray. Now, with the hearth-fires of Jerusalem all around him, the nearest safe retreat was that little grove of trees just beyond the eastern wall.

Gethsemane was more than just a personal retreat, though. It was also an invitation to his friends. This was where he asked them to stay awake, to accompany him, to watch and pray. And I, too, found that I was invited to come to the Savior at Gethsemane, and pray.

We entered past a black-painted gate, emblazoned with the bright red cross of the old Kingdom of Jerusalem, and stepped into a hushed garden lost to time. Traffic whizzed by on a major road just outside, and tourists marched up and down the stairs of the adjoining church, but their sounds faded into a soft murmur in the presence of the ancient, gray-leaved trees. There was a wizened solemnity about them—their twisting, gnarled trunks, and the way their leafy limbs seemed to be uplifted in prayer. The trees themselves looked like a man lifting desperate pleas to the heavens: sprawled out on the ground at their bases, and raising arms to the sky above.

The trees in that garden were hundreds of years old, and perhaps a thousand, but Norah told us that many of them grew out of the old stumps of former trees—still to be seen today—and that those stumps were many hundreds of years older still. It was possible, then, that this was the spot, and these the trees, that played witness to Christ's agony in the night before he died. The name of the place itself—Gethsemane—marked its identity as an olive grove; the name derives from the practice of using stones of tremendous weight to crush the olives for their oil (an example of which we had seen back in Nazareth Village); and it was here, in "the garden of crushing," that our Lord was pressed down in prayer under the enormous weight of the world's sin and pain.

For some reason, I had always imagined Jesus just praying in a dark grove, surrounded by trees, and perhaps looking up to the sky as he pleaded with his Father. But when one actually stands there, in that garden on the lower slopes of the Mount of Olives, it's clear that the Temple would have dominated the view. If one turns toward the city at all, it is the mighty wall of the Temple Mount that commands one's vision, and the Temple itself, standing taller than the Dome of the Rock now does, would have stood out against the sky in its white-sided, gold-gilt splendor. In that moment of agony, Christ likely would have looked there—toward the doors that led to the Holy of Holies, and to the open face of his Father. No doubt there was comfort and consolation in seeing the beauty of that place, where the glory of the divine presence rested in the midst of Israel. But there also would have been a confirmation of his mission: for there, standing before the great doors that led to the holiest place, stood the altar of sacrifice. As Christ gazed into the Temple courts that night in Jerusalem, praying from the darkness of the garden, he would have seen, between himself and the Holy of Holies, the fiery altar where the blood of the Passover lambs would be poured out. The cup of the Passover sacrifice would have to be drunk before he could enter the glory of his Father's presence again.

———·———

We walked around the garden for a while in quiet devotion, then turned our steps to the church. We knew that our schedule promised us more time in Gethsemane the next morning, so we felt no need to cling to the peaceful silence of the garden. By the time we climbed up to the pillared portico of the church, the golden sunlight of late afternoon was slipping away toward evening. Sunday was coming to a close in Jerusalem.

The church beside Gethsemane, the Basilica of the Agony, is run by the Franciscans, but it has embraced a spirit of Christian inclusion inspired by Christ's prayer in that spot, "that they might all be one" (John 17:21). So it's called "The Church of All Nations," and its twelve domes include intricate symbols of the countries of the world. The pillars and mosaic on the outer façade make it one of the most beautiful and recognizable churches in the world. Enshrined in its altar area, behind a low wrought-iron fence, is the great rock of Gethsemane itself, upon which Jesus is said to have cast himself down in the soul-stricken pain of his prayers.

I was expecting our stop at the Church of All Nations to be the same as all of our other church tours: we were often running short on time, so we would have to hustle in and out of many magnificent places of worship in ten or fifteen minutes in order to maximize the number of Israel's wonders that we would get to see. It was usually just enough time to have a quick glance around, snap a few pictures, listen to Norah's narration, and then move on. But a remarkable thing happened. Gethsemane had been the last stop on our itinerary for the day, and by some miraculous happenstance, we had more time than we anticipated. So our leaders told us that we would have time enough to rest and pray in the place of Christ's own prayer. And then it got even better. My heart leapt as soon as we stepped in the doorway. A Franciscan friar was there, holding a finger to his lips to remind all the tourists to be quiet in the church, because a worship service had begun.

Now, to remind the reader why this was so profoundly joyful for me, one has to remember my desire to participate in a real service of worship in one of the churches of the Holy Land. Many of the most powerful moments of my life had come as I joined in corporate worship with the people of God in the various lands of my sojourning: from evensong in Canterbury Cathedral to a quiet meeting of a persecuted church in Sudan, and from an Easter processional in a Tanzanian basilica to a Ukrainian house church packed with Roma Gypsies. I had wished for a chance to enter a flesh-and-blood meeting of the Christians of Israel as they gathered to perform together the praiseful work of the liturgies they had raised for two thousand years. But from the beginning, it had been clear that my desires would not come to fruition: I had not voiced my hope in the planning stages, and now there was simply no time in our schedule to add a church service without cutting out a once-in-a-lifetime visit to a Gospel site.

But then, on Sunday in Jerusalem, I was given my place at a worship service. Once again, it felt as if God had been preparing this moment as a gift for me, so precisely and beautifully did it match the heart-cry of my desires. While my friends walked about the church and studied its beautiful domes, I slipped into a seat in the nave and drank in the worship of the people of God like a thirst-crazed man slaking his soul at a well both deep and cool.

It was a Catholic liturgy, part of the regular cycle of worship practiced by the community of faith at Gethsemane, and it happened to be in Latin, but I knew enough of the service to follow the movement of its prayers and to twine my heart together with the ancient words. My great desire could not have found a more fitting resolution.

With tear-swimming eyes I sat and prayed, thanking God for that moment and for the chance to be part of his company of saints in Jerusalem. As the liturgy ended, they opened the gate in the fence by the altar. My pilgrimage group was already filtering back outside, and none of them thought to take the opportunity that I seized in that moment. Following a few others from the worshiping congregation, I walked up to the front of the church, knelt down where medieval pilgrims and early church fathers had knelt before me, and reverently placed a hand against the rock of my Lord's agony. That very rock, if the traditions are true, had felt the touch of his blood-wracked sweat as he wrestled with the pain it would cost to secure my salvation. And by the time he rose from that stone, and turned to meet the arresting mob, he had bowed his heart to the Father's plan: he had chosen the pain, had chosen me and all nations, and had set his face toward the cross. As I worshiped there on that Sunday in Jerusalem, and as I touched the stone on which he bled and prayed for me and all believers, I felt that he had chosen me again, and had welcomed me to his embrace.

DOWN INTO THE DARKNESS

I love my God, but with no love of mine, for I have
    none to give;
I love thee, Lord, but all the love is thine; for by thy
    life I live.
I am as nothing, and rejoice to be
Emptied, and lost, and swallowed up in thee.

        —Madame Guyon, "I Love My God"

After Jesus' betrayal and arrest in Gethsemane, he was
brought to stand trial in the middle of the night at the house
of Caiaphas the high priest. Today a church marks the spot, called
the church of Saint Peter in Gallicantu. It's one of the many lovely
twentieth-century pilgrim chapels built around the Holy Land,
resting on sites long venerated by Christians for their connections to the story of Jesus. This particular church sits on the slope

of Zion's hill, toward the southern end of the Old City, where many wealthy and priestly families had their homes. There are many clues pointing to this spot as the location of Caiaphas' house, a high priestly manor in which Jewish religious and judicial business could be carried out without having to go up to the Temple courts. Archaeological excavations have indicated that the deep cisterns beneath the house were used as holding cells during the first century—that is, as a place to keep religious prisoners before handing them over to Roman justice or dealing with them under the Sanhedrin's own authority.

Adjoining the courtyard of the church are the remains of an old Roman-era roadway, tracing just beside the church and down across the central valley toward the City of David. Norah told us that that road was very likely the one that Jesus would have walked on his way from the Last Supper to the Garden of Gethsemane. It was the main avenue running eastward from the hill of Zion, and so Jesus and the disciples would have walked across those very stones, beneath the glowering walls of the high priestly palace, and then out into the night toward the lower slopes of the Mount of Olives. And so I took a moment to stand there, my feet against the ancient stones where Jesus would have stepped.

One of the main features of the site, aside from that roadway, is the courtyard. A broad, square flagstone yard adjoins the lower floor of the church, and it is here that a monument stands to the story of Peter's repeated disavowal of Christ. In the Gospels, Jesus is taken from the Garden of Gethsemane, back up the very roadway he had walked earlier that night, and brought within the house of Caiaphas to answer the questions of the high priest and his council. While he is on trial, Peter, who has trailed along at a safe distance after running away in the garden, takes up a spot in the courtyard. Here he is confronted by three people who claim to recognize him as being connected with Jesus, and each time, Peter violently denies any knowledge of his master. This was the sorrowful denial that Jesus himself had foretold a few hours earlier, and now it was coming true. At the sound of the cock-crow, Peter remembers what Jesus has said, and, overcome with shame, he goes out and weeps.

Today, in the courtyard of the Church of Saint Peter in Gallicantu, is a statue of Peter's betrayal, crowned with the rooster itself. Before we walked into the church, I marveled at the way that even Peter's most-regretted failing had become a thing of beauty under the message of God's grace. I rather hoped that no one would ever be building statues that described my darkest sins, nor erecting churches to mark the spots of my failures and humiliations. But on the other hand, that's what grace is all about, isn't it?—that despite the shame of the sin itself, the overarching story of that place (as well as of our lives) is in fact a story of the beauty of God's redemption, even in (and perhaps especially in) our darkest moments.

The church itself is small, as many of these pilgrim chapels are, but in this case, most pilgrims aren't coming to see the sanctuary. The real attraction, the reason why people flock to the site, is below: the cistern underneath, called the Prison of Christ. If indeed the place is the site of the Gospel story, as many indications suggest, then the cistern is likely the place where Jesus spent part of the last night before his crucifixion. After the priestly trial concluded, they would have locked him down there while they waited to take him to Pontius Pilate in the morning. Those hours in Jesus' life are not narrated in the Gospels, but logic would suggest that the story played out that way, and there are ancient Christian traditions which say that that is exactly what happened.

So down we went, following the stairway into the dimness of underground passageways where long lines of other pilgrims waited in silence for their turn to enter the place of Jesus' desolation. In the small room before the descent into the cistern, there's a hauntingly beautiful statue of Jesus, a tortured prisoner bound and on his knees, but looking up in prayer. Before being cast down into the dark emptiness of the earth for what remained of the night, he was beaten and mocked by the Temple guards, and the statue imagines what he might have looked like in that moment.

Just as in the Church of the Nativity, we were able to beg our way into attaching ourselves onto a larger group of pilgrims. This time, we accompanied a group of Asian pilgrims. In reverent quietness, we all descended the stairway down into the cistern. It was not a large space, though it might have seemed cavernous to a single prisoner who landed there in the darkness: with about thirty of us down there, we were shoulder-to-shoulder in the dimness of the place. It was deep, though: easily the height of several men from top to bottom. I felt like I was standing in the belly of the earth. I stooped down and pressed my hand against the dust in the bottom of the cistern.

Around us were signs of ancient Christian veneration: old ochre-paint Byzantine crosses, still just visible on the walls. There was a slight chill to the place, like the damp, earthy coolness of a root cellar. I thought about Jesus, locked in the pitch blackness of this place, bruised and alone. Just a few hours before, he had longed for his disciples' companionship in the Garden of Gethsemane, had wanted them to watch and pray with him as he entered his agonies there. What must he have felt now, having seen them all fleeing at his arrest, and then having been locked away in the pit of the earth, despised and rejected? For a prisoner under judgment, the cistern was a chilling presage of the grave. There in the darkness of the deep well of his sorrow, I was reminded that my Lord knew the hurts and lonelinesses of life in all their heart-rending poignancy: he was, as the old prophet had said, "a man of suffering, and familiar with pain" (Is. 53:3).

The priest that accompanied the larger group of pilgrims stepped up to a lectern, which was the only furniture in the otherwise untouched and ancient cistern. There was a Bible there, standing open to Psalm 88. That passage, often interpreted by the early church as a prophecy of this particular moment in the life of Christ, is read aloud by each group of pilgrims that enters the cistern. And as the words rolled around me, echoing softly off the earthen walls, I could hear the weight of Jesus' sorrow.

> I am overwhelmed with troubles and my life draws near to
>   death.
> I am counted among those who go down to the pit; I am like
>   one without strength.
> I am set apart with the dead, like the slain who lie in the grave,
> Whom you remember no more, who are cut off from your care.
> You have put me in the lowest pit, in the darkest depths…
> You have taken from me my closest friends and have made me
>   repulsive to them.
> I am confined and cannot escape; my eyes are dim with grief…
> You have taken from me friend and neighbor—darkness is my
>   closest friend.
>
> (Ps. 88:3-6, 8-9, 18)

TAKING UP MY CROSS

Take the cross as an indestructible foundation, and
build all other articles of faith upon it.

—Cyril of Jerusalem, Catechesis 13

We were down to our last day in Jerusalem. I awoke with a
strange mixture of excitement and dread: excitement for
the sights that lay ahead, including the one I had most longed to
see, the Church of the Holy Sepulchre, but dread at the increas-
ingly likely possibility that our schedule would force us to rush
hastily in and out of that ancient church without time to pause or
pray. I had pressed Josh, in his rearrangement of the schedule, to
make sure we wouldn't slight the Holy Sepulchre, the one place
that for ages past had been the defining stop of a true pilgrimage:
for travelers, crusaders, and wandering saints, anything less would
have counted as a pale half-measure. "It's the most important
place in the history of the world," I said—and I believe that it is

just that, because of the cosmic, history-shattering significance of Jesus' death and resurrection—so it would have been a disappointment to have to throw it merely a passing glance, like just another check-mark on our itinerary.

Our schedule had us beginning the day by walking the whole of the Via Dolorosa ("Way of Sorrow"), with the Church of the Holy Sepulchre as its end-point, and then going to a fixed appointment at the Garden Tomb, a Protestant site thought by some pilgrims to be a rival claimant to the title of Jesus' burial-ground. The fact that the Holy Sepulchre was sandwiched between an event that seemed likely to run long, and another event with an immovable start-time, did not assuage my fears.

But I tried to brush all that aside, and go into our final day in Jerusalem with a sense of humility and openness, to embrace whatever God had for me. So we started out early, walking through the Muslim Quarter of the Old City until we came to the Catholic monastery grounds that marked the beginning of the traditional Via Dolorosa: the route that Jesus had long been thought to walk from his trial to his crucifixion. We entered the city early enough that the peaceful magic of the sunrise hours lingered in the air: quiet, empty streets greeted us, and there was a stillness to the city.

The first set of stops on the Via Dolorosa are within the grounds of the Catholic monastery, where two chapels commemorate Christ's sufferings under Pilate's guards at his trial. While that spot did stand adjacent to the old Roman garrison, it is now the near-unanimous consensus among scholars that this is not where Jesus had been put on trial. Rather, that most likely occurred in the western part of the city, where Roman officials held court at the Herodian palace complex during their infrequent visits to Jerusalem—which means, naturally, that the whole route of the traditional Via Dolorosa is nothing more than a pious fiction. Nonetheless, honored as it is by time and by the memories and prayers of many faithful pilgrims who've walked that path before, each group still walks the route from Antonia to the tomb, remembering Jesus' sorrows along the way.

Like many other pilgrim groups, we rented a wooden cross at the first station, and then began our long walk through the Old City of Jerusalem. Though we didn't stop at every one of the traditional fourteen "Stations of the Cross," we paused every now and then to hold one of our mini-services of prayer, with Josh giving poignant recitations of the story of Jesus' passion. At each stop, I would lead the group in singing a verse of the old spiritual "Were You There When They Crucified My Lord?"—a song which, whenever I hear it now, brings me back to the narrow alleys and market-stalls of the Via Dolorosa. I ticked off the Stations of the Cross as we walked by them; occasionally we would stop at one for a moment's rest. We also paused at an archaeological site along the way, which featured the underground foundations of the old Fortress Antonia, and again beneath the famous Ecce Homo arch, from which Pilate had been imagined to have proclaimed "Behold the man!" at his final judgment over Jesus.

On the second half of our walk down the Via Dolorosa, it came to my turn to carry the cross. It was heavier than I expected. Beneath its weight, I wove my way through the now-crowded streets of Jerusalem. The route was commonly full of pilgrims, but it was also a normal set of streets and alleys, filled with all the passersby, residents, and sidewalk merchants one might expect. This seemed fitting to me: the call to take up one's cross and follow Jesus is not something that takes place far away from the world of everyday life, but in the very middle of our busy existences, full of neighbors, jobs, buying and selling, traveling and rest. So there, in the middle of the bustling world, I carried my cross for Jesus.

It also struck me as fitting in another way: though I knew, historically speaking, that this was almost certainly not the real route that Jesus walked to Calvary, it was not Jesus' cross that I was called to bear. When he asked his disciples to take up the cross and follow, it was each disciple's own cross that he spoke of—the love-sorrowing cost of following a crucified Lord (Matt. 16:24). And when the book of Hebrews speaks of the call of discipleship, it exhorts us to go outside the city to the place of his disgrace (Heb. 13:13)— not to walk his own pathway, for there is but one atoning passion, Christ's alone, which we cannot replicate—but to walk our own journey to meet him there. We all trace our own pilgrimages to Christ, from many different places and through many different ways, but we all meet him at one and the same spot: the rugged rock of Calvary, where his sacrifice and our journeys always intersect.

We came to the ninth Station of the Cross, the last one outside the Church of the Holy Sepulchre. We leaned our cross in the corner of the street and looked in soaring expectation toward the rising domes of the church. As we stood there, we sang "Were You There?" one last time. It called to my memory a dear church lady who had passed away the year before, Judy, old and long impaired with mental disabilities, who had loved that hymn and sang it with gusto at nearly every one of our music-based "singspiration" services. It's not quite right to say that her mental disabilities impaired her, though—rather, they clarified her spirit into the sort of loving simplicity which those of us with more complicated lives could only regard as beautiful and saintly. She had walked her journey—a very different journey than mine—and was now with her Lord. But for both her and me, though our pathways were different, they both intersected in the unshakable reality of what had happened at the place that stood in front of me now: the spot where my life, and hers, and those of a billion other saints, had met the Master at the foot of the cross.

THE SORROW OF GOLGOTHA

Christ the Life of all the living,
Christ the death of Death our foe,
Who Thyself for us once giving
To the darkest depths of woe,
Didst Thou die for me to win
Rescue from the bonds of sin:
Thousand, thousand thanks shall be
Blessèd Jesus, brought to Thee.

—Ernst C. Homburg, "Jesu, Meines Lebens Leben"

Every now and then, in the course of life and ministry, I get to share my testimony of faith with a group of fellow Christians—the story of when and how I was saved. And sometimes, when the opportunity arises, I choose to start with an important theological point: "The story of my salvation does not begin with me or my childhood prayer of faith. I was saved two thousand years ago, on the hill of Calvary." Now, on that bright morning in Jerusalem, I found myself standing in front of that very spot—the place where Christ had won my salvation, the place my whole life's journey revolved around, like the Earth to the Sun. This was the moment I had been waiting for with heart-aching hopes. Though I hadn't set high emotional expectations for any other spot on our pilgrimage itinerary, whenever I had imagined this particular place, the thought was instantly met with a rush of tears.

As I had feared, our time looked like it would be shorter than I hoped to have there. But now I was here, and with the place itself before me, those old fears melted away in the grandness of the moment. We entered the courtyard that stood beside the church, where the main entrance was nestled in the corner between the nave and the transept. It was a huge, old, complicated church, but I had already studied maps and pictures of its layout, so I knew what to expect.

The Church of the Holy Sepulchre can often present a bewildering (and in some cases, distasteful) experience to pilgrims, but if you know a little about the place and its arrangement, it takes on a wild and mystifying sort of charm. One of the things the church is well known for, aside from enclosing the traditional sites for both Jesus' death and resurrection, is that it is jointly managed by a handful of ancient denominations that are constantly competing, sometimes in tremendously acrimonious ways, against one another's claims on the place. But that didn't bother me much—it seemed oddly appropriate, in a way, that the church of Jesus' death and resurrection should be rather like a portrait in miniature of the global church—sometimes divided by silly and stupid quarrels, but still, in a mystery of grace, forming a single, grand, beautiful community of faith with one another.

The first thing I looked for, before even entering the church, was a little stairway to a small chapel up on the right, which commemorated an ancient pilgrim whose story had blessed the shape of my own journey. Mary of Egypt, a young prostitute living in Alexandria back in the days of the old Byzantine Empire, had decided to join a group going on pilgrimage to Jerusalem. She had done it in a spirit of mockery, as a bit of a jest, and had paid for her way by seducing various other pilgrims as she went. When she finally reached this spot, though, standing before the doors of the Church of the Holy Sepulchre, she had felt both an overwhelming desire to go inside, yet also a crushing awareness of her own sin and unworthiness. As the story goes, the Lord had mercy on her, and in a single moment, as her heart-cry of despairing faith reached out to him, he cleansed her of her life of sin. In fervent repentance, she dedicated the remainder of her days to God, serving him as a wandering prayer warrior of the Judean wilderness: one of the greatest desert mothers of them all. Her story spoke to my own deep desire for transformation; it gave hope to my dream that God might somehow have mercy on me by giving me such a spirit of unflagging thirst for holiness that nothing could ever stand in the way of that pursuit again.

We passed beneath the great doorway and entered the church. Ahead of us was a group of women kneeling by the stone associated with Jesus' preparation for burial, and I knew that just to my right were the stairs that led up to Golgotha. To the left, I also knew, was the great round rotunda where the edicule stood: the little church-within-a-church that housed Jesus' empty tomb.

We turned right, climbed the narrow stairway to the chapel there, commemorating Jesus' crucifixion on Calvary, and joined the back of the line of those waiting to kneel down and touch the ground beneath the altar. Many Protestant pilgrims rue the fact that Calvary looks absolutely nothing like they imagined it: encased within a church, you would never know that it was anything other than an upper story of the building unless you were told so. But we, in our desire for preserving the original state of things, are simply seeing things through the lens of our own culture; many previous generations of Christians thought it a far finer thing to surround and encase the most precious places of Jesus' life with grand and beautiful monuments. So you have to use your imagination a bit to remember that you are now standing atop what was once a hill that lay just beyond the city gates in the crook of Jerusalem's wall, and to see in the gold-edged icons of the chapel a reflection of the glory of what Jesus did there.

So amid the dark stones of the ancient church, we waited. The line moved slowly, ever so slowly. I drank in the beauty of the artwork over and around me while I waited, watching each pilgrim stoop down and reach beneath the altar, to where the old rocky surface of Golgotha could still be felt. And it was just then that Josh came up beside me with an apologetic expression on his face. "Sorry, Matt—we're going to have to leave as soon as we're through with this line. We have to make our appointment at the Garden Tomb, or else we'll lose our spot." I groaned inwardly. To leave the Church of the Holy Sepulchre without ever having even stepped into sight of the edicule of Jesus' tomb!—

it was a heart-sinking blow. The one place I had most wanted to see—the place I would have traded seeing all the others for—was being ripped away from me. Josh gave an apologetic pledge that he would try to make sure we could return later on, but I felt that such chances were slight foundations on which to set one's hope; particularly since we had several other sites on our itinerary after the Garden Tomb.

Feeling suddenly desolate and forlorn, I approached the altar of Golgotha. In a way, it was just right, though—to have to let go of my own fleeting hopes, to be forced to let die an imagined future that I had clung to with great desire—it was just a small piece of the far greater sorrow and despair that Jesus' followers would have known as they stood on Calvary. I looked at the icon of Christ crucified, hanging there before my eyes, and thought of his pain-wracked sacrifice on the cross—the climactic act of his endless love, which overturned the universe and poured grace into my soul. And then I knelt down, reached beneath the altar, and put my hand down into the hole. There my fingers brushed the craggy stone on which his blood had been poured out; there, kneeling at the foot of the cross, I had finally arrived at the place I had long told people about: the place where I was saved two thousand years ago.

Back in Roman days, Golgotha had stood in the middle of an old quarry. Before that section became engulfed in the ever-growing city, its stone was cut for use in building projects. There was one section of poorer-grade stone, however, that had been left standing in the quarry, and that formed the little hill of Golgotha. It was, quite literally, "the stone the builders rejected," just as the prophecy of Psalm 118:22 had said. That stone had become the cornerstone of my life—I had felt the foundations of my existence; I had come for the first time to this spot, in the middle of an ancient city thousands of miles from my home, and found that I had known the place all along.

THE PROMISE OF RESURRECTION

Arise! He who commands it is the Resurrection. For the Savior becomes all things to all people everywhere: bread for the hungry, water for the thirsty, resurrection for the dead, a physician for the sick, redemption for sinners.

—Cyril of Jerusalem, "Homily on the Paralytic by the Pool"

I went to the Garden Tomb—a Protestant site just north of the Old City, discovered and established in the nineteenth century—and I was feeling just slightly irked and resentful. The place annoyed me at first, because our appointment there had pulled me away from the one place I really wanted to be: the Church of the Holy Sepulchre. I was also, after some significant research into the matter, convinced of the fact that the Holy Sepulchre had a vastly better claim of being the historic site of Jesus' empty tomb.

Nonetheless, I tried to change my attitude. I had lived a full and joyous life without ever having seen the entirety of the Church of the Holy Sepulchre, so if I were destined to spend the rest of my days that way, it was far from the worst of fates. Besides, this stop at the Garden Tomb was the intended climax of our fellowship as a pilgrimage group: to take communion together, here near the end of our journey, after walking the way of sorrow to the cross, and now surrounded by the verdant loveliness of this reminder of Jesus' resurrection. I didn't want to have my forlorn regrets weighing down a moment like that, so I tried to trundle all of that emotional baggage to the back of my mind as we strolled through the garden.

It was indeed a lovely spot: full of lush greenery that makes it stand out from the dry, stony city around. Our guide brought us around to the far side of the complex, where a little wooden palisade overlooked a Palestinian bus station. But it wasn't the bus station that one was meant to look at; it was the rise just behind, whose craggy, dusty features, if one screwed one's eyes just right and used a liberal amount of imagination, came to resemble a human skull.

To a good nineteenth-century Protestant, to whom the Church of the Holy Sepulchre would seem a disheartening labyrinth of gold-fringed superstition, and who knew his Bible well enough to recall that Golgotha meant "the place of the skull," the possibility suggested by this place was irresistible. Perhaps this lonely hill, just beyond the walls of the city, was the real Calvary itself, the mount of crucifixion. So the property adjoining "Skull Hill" (also referred to as "Gordon's Calvary") was bought up and developed, including a marvelous discovery on the other side of the plot: a well-preserved ancient tomb, bearing inside an old Christian graffito etched on the wall. While I admit that I (like most scholars) am dubious of any possible connection between this site and the passion events, even I could see the power of the place as a way to enter into the story of Jesus' death and resurrection. Its power was more evocative than historical. Even if this were not the spot, it likely did look very much like this; and for anyone who would rather imagine it as it was, this spot was a fair deal more accessible than the monument-encrusted Church of the Holy Sepulchre.

We finished our tour around the site, taking a moment to enter the tomb itself. I looked at the empty shelf where the body would have lain, and smiled. Just as it didn't really matter that we had walked the wrong route for the Via Dolorosa, so it didn't matter if we might end up standing in the wrong site for the resurrection. In the same way that carrying the cross is for us just as it was for Jesus—our own cross, on our own journey, in imitation of our Master—so also the resurrection was not just for Jesus, but for us too.

This second empty tomb came to be a reminder of that for me. In my case, the Holy Sepulchre was the place that brought me into the immediacy of the story of Jesus' resurrection, and this second tomb, tucked away in the garden discovered and nurtured by my own spiritual forebears—Protestant heroes like Horatio Spafford and Charles Gordon—this place made me think of my own resurrection. The promise was for me—that one day, because of Jesus, I would be raised in triumph over the grave. More than that: Ephesians tells us that even now, the resurrection-power of God, the same power that raised Jesus from the tomb, is at work in us (Eph. 1:19–20). I stepped out of the Garden Tomb, out of the dimness and into the light of flowers and birds and trees, and I felt a gentle swell of gratitude and peace. I had seen the emptiness of death's threats and the abundant fullness of eternal life, vouchsafed to me in Christ.

We retired to a shady nook of the garden fitted out with benches, where a communion set had been prepared for us. There we held our final service of prayer together, we eleven pilgrims far from home, and when we partook the symbols of Christ's body and blood, it was a declaration of the communion that Christ had wrought among us. To take communion anywhere is a holy and powerful thing; to take it in Jerusalem, together with fellow pilgrims who have shared many roads and many prayers, is a marvel of delight.

———·———

In my Baptist tradition, we treasure the practice of communion. But at times, we unintentionally diminish its importance in our efforts to make clear that we're not Catholics. Our theology tries to set its foundations squarely on the authority of Scripture alone, and it has found no compelling biblical reason to believe in transubstantiation, the Catholic dogma which holds that the bread and wine actually become, in a very literal sense, the body and blood of Christ. However, in reacting against the Catholic position (as well as other church traditions that hold a sacramental view), we sometimes say that communion is "just a symbol."

I'm fine with calling it a symbol, but I'm not fine with the "just," as if we're trying to downplay expectations for what this ritual means. Symbols can be mighty things, speaking to the deepest hopes of our hearts and the highest truths of our faith. I've seen grown men weep at the sight of symbols (like the US flag, for one). They bear tremendous meaning, and shape us in a way that words and thought alone cannot.

Take, for instance, the other great biblical symbol for the body of Christ— the church itself, the community of Christians. Over and over again, the apostle Paul comes back to this image of the church as the body of Christ. We understand the power and meaning of this, because Paul spells it out so clearly in his teaching: it speaks to the deeply interconnected way that we exist as a community of faith. You won't hear many Baptists arguing that the language of "the Body of Christ" is just a symbol, in a way that diminishes its importance, because we know that that symbol stands at the core of our life together. If we can believe in the unity of the Body of Christ as something real, practical, and deeply meaningful, then we ought to carry the same sort of "symbolic" view to our celebration of the body of Christ as revealed in communion.

Consider for a moment how the Jews of Jesus' day received his teaching on what we call communion—in his words, eating his flesh and drinking his blood. It certainly doesn't strike them as just another ordinance, another rule for a pious act to check off our list every month. They react as if he has said something wild, bizarre, and even repulsive (John 6:51–60). This is not a symbol you would invent unless it carried deep meanings for those involved.

So why does Jesus use this particular act? Why does he choose a symbol of eating flesh and drinking blood? One possible answer, illuminated at the Last Supper, which took place during the Passover festival, is that these are symbols of sacrifice. The language he uses of his body ("given for you") and his blood ("poured out for you") are phrases that recall the Temple practice of offering sacrifices for sin and guilt. Part of the Temple ritual was that the priests who presented these offerings would eat the meat of the sacrificial animals (Lev. 6:24–7:6). In this sense, Jesus is inviting us, in taking the bread of communion, to participate as recipients of his act of sacrifice on our behalf, just as the priests did in ancient Israel.

But what about the blood? If you know your Bibles well, then you know that drinking blood was definitely not part of the Temple rituals. In fact, it is specifically forbidden several times in the Old Testament, and the reason why it is forbidden is because "the life of every creature is its blood" (Lev. 17:10–14; Deut. 12:23–34). Why, then, does Jesus break this clear taboo listed in the Law of God by telling people to drink his blood? It seems that he has chosen this symbol with the shock value of that very taboo in mind: you must drink his blood, because that is the only source of true life (John 6:53–54). It is a symbol not just of receiving his sacrifice, but of being joined to his very life. Drinking wine or juice at communion signifies our reception of the indwelling, eternal life of communion with God. And it is the life of Christ himself, to whom we are united in faith, which grants us the resurrection power of which Paul speaks in Ephesians 1:19–20, just as Jesus promised: "Whoever eats my flesh and drinks my blood has eternal life, and I will raise them up at the last day" (John 6:54).

————·————

As we left the Garden Tomb, my thoughts went back again to Horatio Spafford, one of the site's earliest supporters. The lines of his famous hymn echoed through my mind as I thought about Christ's victory over sin and the grave, and the promise of sharing in his resurrection: "My sin—oh, the bliss of this glorious thought!—my sin, not in part, but the whole, is nailed to the cross and I bear it no more: praise the Lord, praise the Lord, O my soul! It is well with my soul; it is well, it is well with my soul!"

AND THEN JESUS CAME IN WITH A WILD SURPRISE

Around [the Sepulchre] holy men had prayed for many generations since Eusebius, and Macarius, and Jerome, and Sabas... Many thousand dying sinners and dying saints in all countries and all times have looked to it with the last straining gaze of their dim eyes, and died with smiling countenances turned toward the tomb... Pilgrims from far lands have laid their burdens down on its rocky floor, and prayers and tears have hallowed it...as the memorial of more earnest faith and adoration than any other spot of ground on this side of the pearl gates.

—William C. Prime, *Tent Life in the Holy Land*

A few years ago, when my oldest son was very small and just learning how to string sentences together, he decided to make up his own "Bible story" after our evening devotional. So my little pajama-clad boy, wiggling with excitement as he talked, told a story of his own invention about Jesus and the disciples. I don't recall much of it now, except for a single line that has always stayed with me: "And then Jesus came in with a wild surprise!" This is the story of the wild surprise that Jesus gave me in Jerusalem.

Our final day had led us all over Jerusalem: from the far end of the Via Dolorosa to the Church of the Holy Sepulchre, where we barely had time to see a single chapel before being pulled out again to go to the Garden Tomb, and after that to several other sites as well. Morning had given way to afternoon, and the end of our day was swiftly approaching. But now, after all those things were done, we saw that there was still some time remaining before we had to be back at the hotel for our farewell dinner. Not a great deal of time, but enough to rectify our earlier haste: we could go back again to the Church of the Holy Sepulchre. I hadn't even dared to put hope in this possibility earlier in the day.

It's a little hard to describe the delight I felt without making it sound a trifle overwrought; but the fact that my dearest hope for the entire trip had been snatched away and then, as if by a work of providential grace, returned—it was the greatest in a long series of winsome surprises that had met me on my pilgrimage. And in this case, it seemed to be so exactly appropriate that it smacked of being staged. What better way, really, to experience the church that houses both Calvary and the empty tomb than to begin by only visiting Calvary, feeling the sorrow of thinking that that's the end, and then later, miraculously being given back the wonder of the whole thing, empty tomb and all? It was rather like seeing, albeit in a very distant and minimal way, the experience of the disciples from their desolation at Calvary to the wild surprise of the empty tomb on Sunday morning.

About half of our group, exhausted by the day's walking, decided not to re-enter the church, but remained sitting on the steps outside to wait for those of us who went back in. This time we turned left inside the main doors, past the place where pilgrims were placing lit prayer-candles to create a little sea of light. Then we strode through the circle of massive pillars that ringed the rotunda, pillars that had stood there from much earlier generations of the church's architecture (all the way back to the Byzantine Empire), and into view of the edicule.

There is no real parallel to the arrangement inside the Church of the Holy Sepulchre; it looks as though someone has built a little church inside a much larger church. Beneath the great dome, with sunlight streaming down upon it, is a little closed-sided chapel of stone, complete with its own steeple, pillars, and inner chapels. It is permitted for pilgrims to go inside the edicule and to spend a moment or two within the tomb of Christ itself. But, as was the case in the Church of the Nativity, the space inside is so small, and the experience in such high demand, that a massive line of pilgrims forms, winding all the way around the back of the edicule and moving forward only by inches and hours. I was breathless with wonder at standing there, beneath the great rotunda. This was the spot where I had imagined myself as I thought ahead to my pilgrimage, and now I was here.

——————

The tomb itself, of course, is not nearly as important as the fact that it is empty. It is the resurrection of Christ, much more than his entombment, that bestows life and meaning on our beliefs. But that doesn't mean his entombment is inconsequential. In many Protestant traditions, we give a lot of attention to Good Friday and Easter Sunday (and, if we're feeling like adding a little extra work for our pastors, we'll throw in Maundy Thursday too). But we scarcely spare a thought for Holy Saturday, the day Jesus' body lay dead in the tomb.

Christian traditions differ on what Jesus' spirit was up to during that time: according to some, he was in paradise (who interpret Luke 23:43 to indicate this), and according to others, he was busy busting down the gates of hell (who believe there's a reference to this in Eph. 4:8–9). But I want to focus on the tomb itself, and Christ's dead body within it. Jesus' "Sabbath rest" on Holy Saturday was, I believe, an indication that God was about to give his "Let there be light" moment for the New Creation to begin.

"On the seventh day, [God] rested from all his work" (Gen. 2:2). Many of us are familiar with this line, part of the closing stanza of Genesis' initial account of creation. After six days of creating, God rested from all his work. The passage goes on to say that God blessed the seventh day and made it holy, because that was the day of his rest. But stop for a moment and ask a very basic question: Why? Why would God have to rest? Did he get worn out from all the hard work of designing a universe? Granted, it does seem a difficult task, but if we believe what Christian theology has taught us, that God is unbounded and omnipotent, then he should be able to create an infinity of multiverses without ever being taxed at all.

Perhaps, one might answer, it's just a poetic way of saying, "And then after six days, God stopped creating stuff." It doesn't have to imply that God needed a rest. There's just one problem, though—if the passage only intended to say that God stopped working after six days, it strikes one as a little odd that such significance is poured into the seventh day: "God blessed the seventh day and made it holy" (Gen. 2:3). This suggests that there is something important about what God did on the seventh day, not merely a marker of what he didn't do. If it was intended to mark the end of creative activity, we might have expected him to bless the sixth day, not the seventh, just as we celebrate the day of World War I's ending (Nov. 11), not the day after it ended.

Some contemporary scholars have floated another theory, based on the fact that the terminology of a divine figure "resting" was associated with temple language in the ancient Near East. In this view (of which I think there is serious merit), Genesis 1-2 is portraying the entire cosmos as a great creation-temple of God, in which he will dwell among his creatures (a vision restored and consummated in the last pages of Scripture, Rev. 21–22). Thus, the meaning of God's rest would have to do with his "taking up residence" in his creation-temple and enjoying the fruits of his labors. But while there's certainly something to this, it can't be the whole story, because the Old Testament so closely aligns God's Sabbath rest in creation with the command for humans to rest as well.

Another possible answer that sometimes gets put out there is that God rested on the seventh day not for his own sake, but for ours. God knew that it would be spiritually profitable and physically healthy for us to take one day in seven to rest and to spend time focusing on him, and so he inaugurated the Sabbath in order that we might have a pattern to follow. There's some merit to this argument. After all, in the Gospels Jesus himself says, "The Sabbath was made for mankind" (Mark 2:27). But there are still some loose threads to this argument. Within the context of the Old Testament, it does not seem that God would have had to actually take a Sabbath for himself just in order to make it a permanent practice for humanity. After all, God gives lots of binding laws to his people without performing them beforehand himself. It's interesting to note that when we are commanded to keep the Sabbath in the Ten Commandments, the explicit reason given is not "because it's good for you," but because "[God] rested on the seventh day" (Ex. 20:11). In many locations in the Old Testament, God describes the practice as "my Sabbath," and as "the Sabbath, holy to the Lord." So despite the good sense that arises from suggesting that the Sabbath-rest of God was always simply meant for our well-being, the Bible itself consistently implies that the Sabbath means something for God; it is done in reference to him.

So we come back to the original question: Why did God rest on the seventh day of creation? Well, as it happens, there is a parallel event in the Gospels: the one full Sabbath-day that Jesus was dead and buried in his tomb. This was the day of his "rest," after his labors were complete on the cross: the day we call Holy Saturday in church tradition (or, to use biblical language, it probably ought to be called "the Holy Sabbath Day"). Perhaps God rested on the seventh day after creation in order to prefigure and foreshadow the resting of Christ in the tomb on Holy Saturday.

The marvelous thing, though, is that it doesn't end there. When we link the Sabbath to the life and death of Christ, a slight shift in meaning takes place. The Sabbath is no longer an end in itself, a rest for the sake of rest; it now becomes a pause before something even bigger: the New Creation. On Sunday morning, Jesus Christ rose from the dead and unleashed God's work of New Creation. Here and now, in Christ Jesus, God is actively at work re-creating his masterpiece from the inside out, wiping away the stain of sin and making us what we were always meant to be. The process of New Creation is a mirrored image of the pattern of the first creation: instead of ending with mankind, it starts with mankind. If a person comes to Jesus Christ, there the New Creation is at work (2 Cor. 5:17). The apostle Paul even hints that not only humanity, but all of creation will one day share in the liberation from bondage that comes as a result of this New Creation inaugurated by Christ's resurrection (Romans 8:19–21).

In a sense, then, the Sabbath was God's pause in his creative work between the end of the Old Creation and the beginning of his New Creation. It was the period in which, just as Christ was dead on Holy Saturday, mankind was dead in their sins before being brought back to life through Jesus Christ. God's Sabbath-rest was anticipatory, looking forward to the real event: the Resurrection and the re-creation of humanity in Christ. This, incidentally, is why the early Christians gave up worshiping on Saturday: not because they thought it was a trifling thing to disregard one of the Ten Commandments, but because they realized that the meaning of the Old Testament Sabbath was not really about the Sabbath itself: it had always been pointing to something else, to the next day, the dawning of God's New Creation. So, in honor of the true meaning of Sabbath, they worshiped on "the eighth day" (as the early church fathers would often refer to it), the first day of the new week of God's creation. The Sabbath, then, was not just rest for rest's sake. It was a foreshadowing of what God was going to do in Jesus Christ. God rested on the seventh day, just as Jesus rested in death on the seventh day. The Sabbath has always been pointing forward: not an ending, but a pause before the greatest work of all began anew.

———·———

As we joined the vast line and began waiting for our turn to enter, a strange thing happened. I was delighted, so delighted, to be there, but it suddenly struck me as a light and little thing, of vanishingly small importance compared to the living reality of what had happened there. Over and over through my mind, the words of Luke 24:5–6 were sounding like a trumpet. It was the question of the angels on Easter morning: "Why do you seek the living among the dead? He is not here, he is risen!" I looked around the line of people waiting to get in, saw the mix of weariness, joy, and expectation in their faces. I thought briefly about trying to start a chorus of "Christ the Lord is Risen Today," but thought it better to keep the trumpets in my soul to myself, and let quiet awe reign in the cathedral of the empty tomb.

The line was moving at a barely measurable pace; as our remaining time ticked away, we found we had made it only a quarter of the way around to the entrance. But, having already brought to reality my long-held anticipation of standing in that space, and with the cry of the angels' question ringing through my mind, I didn't feel like I actually had to go inside the tomb itself. For some reason, it had never been part of my expectations for our visit to the church, and so it didn't seem like much of a loss to let it go. And I thought of our weary, footsore friends waiting patiently outside. I knew they would stay there for as long as it took and offer no word of complaint upon our return, but I still thought that it might be the better measure of love not to drag out our stay there to its longest, patience-cracking duration. And if we stayed in line, we would certainly not get to see any of the rest of the massive church, and that was a fate I could not countenance: I, who loved history and loved churches, wanted to drink in as much of the great old place as I could.

So, after a quick discussion with Josh and the others, we left the line. I did manage to peer inside through the single open window in the edicule, into the little antechamber known as the Chapel of the Angels, but I did not go into the tomb itself. Like the apostle John on his first approach, I "looked inside, but did not enter" (Jn. 20:5). I was content with the joy of simply having been there, within the great rotunda that I had dreamed of seeing. With relish and delight, I turned away to make my circuit of the great church, and to drink in its glories.

I had studied enough maps beforehand to know my way around the mind-bending maze of the place. We paused to see the remains of two other first-century tombs that had been unearthed at the site, important evidence that this area had indeed been used for burials in Jesus' day. We peered into the great nave, the seat of the ancient Patriarchate of Jerusalem, where a marker on the floor designates it as the center of the world, and saw the beautiful depiction of Christ, the ruler of all, up in the nave's dome. There's even a chapel that takes you down, far below ground level, where legend has it that Jesus' cross was discovered, buried in that spot, back in the fourth century.

As we walked back out into the bright sunlight of late afternoon, once again I thought of the cry of the angels that had pounded through my heart as we looked at the edicule: "Why do you seek the living among the dead? He is not here; he is risen!" The church was a marvelous memorial to the most important events in my faith; but that's all that it was. The Lord who was crucified there to my left, and whose lifeless body was buried off to my right—that very Lord had risen in triumph on the third day, and now he was alive and rampant in my life.

There's a line from an old play, "The Trial of Jesus," that has stuck with me for some time. The centurion who had overseen Jesus' death is questioned about it after reports of his rising broke out across the city. "Do you believe he is dead?" asks Pilate's wife. "No, lady," responds the centurion, "he is at loose in the world, and nothing will stand against his truth."

BEHOLD OUR END
WHICH IS NO END

O! warm, sweet, tender, even yet
A present help is He;
And faith has still its Olivet,
And love its Galilee.

—John Greenleaf Whittier, "Our Master"

There's an old set of lines from the great church father Augustine, reflecting on death and on heaven, and it ends with this poignant, poetic line: "Behold our end, which is no end." I often use this line when I speak at funerals, but I also think of it sometimes about the end of the Gospels. Here was Jesus, spending a few final days with his disciples before his ascension to the Father's side—it was an end, but, at the same time, it was no end. It was the end of the story of his ministry years with them in Israel, but the beginning of a story far vaster than they could yet imagine.

After the events of Jesus' death and resurrection, the Gospels relate several stories of his interactions with disciples before his ascension. One of the places we visited, back up in Galilee, was associated with these resurrection appearances. It's called Mensa Christi ("Christ's Table"), and it's right on the shore of the lake, not far from Tabgha, where Jesus fed the five thousand. A lovely little church marks the traditional spot of Jesus' breakfast with the disciples and his commissioning of Peter, as told in John 21.

With the haunting trill of a White-throated Kingfisher sounding in the trees high above us, we walked down to the little church and slipped inside. This was another small sanctuary, like so many in Galilee, built for pilgrims rather than congregations. There was an interesting feature to this one, though, in that the broad, rugged rock where Christ was said to have prepared the meal for his disciples was built into the front of the church. Indeed, it dominated the entire forward altar area, and this ancient stone was the object of attention of the only other worshiper in there with us, a Catholic pilgrim who leaned on the rock as he prayed.

My fellow tour-mates looked around for a few moments, then filed back out to walk along the beach. But I lingered back for just a moment. As I had in so many other places, I wanted to use all of my senses to experience the wonder of the Holy Land. So I walked to the front of the church, reached out, and touched the ancient stone. In just that simple act, of letting my fingers take in the rough coarseness of the rock, I felt a bit more connected to the story of what had happened there, as if I, too, had sat around that stone and smelled the roasting fish and smiled to see my Lord once more.

I rejoined the group out on the beach, where they had gathered in the shade of a large tree to do our mini-service. We listened together to the old story: the disciples out in the boat, startled by the stranger on shore directing them into a miraculous catch of fish; Peter so excited that he dove overboard and swam back to meet with Christ; the breakfast of fire-roasted fish on the beach together; and Jesus' long and gentle talk with Peter. "Do you love me?" Jesus asked, over and over again. I held that question in my mind as I cast my eye over the shining blue waters of the lake, over the beach and the church and the statue of Jesus commissioning Peter.

I imagined Peter, having thrice denied Christ, and now thrice given the chance to affirm his love for his Master; and then I thought of myself, and the thousands upon thousands of willful sins that marked my denials and failures as a disciple of the Lord. But there on that shore, I knew as surely as I knew that the sun would keep on shining that the Master I served would give me the chance to affirm my love, even if took thousands upon thousands of times. So the only answer I could give back to his question, there amid the whispers of Galilee's memories, was the same one that Peter gave: "Lord, you know that I love you!"

But there's another part of that interaction in John's account, which does not receive nearly as much attention in sermons and books, but which has stuck with me even more powerfully. As Jesus and Peter are walking along the shore, Peter sees the beloved disciple (traditionally, John) walking along behind, and he asks Jesus, "What about him?" Jesus responds, "If I want him to remain alive until I return, what is that to you? You must follow me" (John 21:22).

We experience the Christian life not only in the vertical dimension of our relationship with Christ, in which we get to pledge him our love and feel the delight of his acceptance. There's also the horizontal dimension of our relationships with one another. Whenever Peter pledges his love, Jesus tells him to feed his sheep and tend his lambs. Our love for Christ will be worked out in practical love toward one another.

But what happens when that horizontal element starts to go awry? What happens when our fellow Christians become not just the ones we're called to love, but the objects of our envy or resentment? We can't know for sure what's really behind Peter's question about the beloved disciple—maybe just simple curiosity about Jesus' plans for John—but to me, in my condition, it always waved the red flag of envy. Sometimes, in my awareness of my sins and my longing for holiness, I find myself looking at other Christians' lives, and the steady, gracious peace that calmly guides their walk with God. "What about that guy, Lord? Why can't my life look and feel more like that?" Or sometimes we see someone who has achieved respect and acclaim that we would have wanted for ourselves, and we are tempted to turn Peter's "What about him?" into a plaintive "But what about me? Why don't I get those things too?" This is the perpetual temptation of our social media age, as we scroll through the happy, glowing reports of our friends' daily lives and inevitably compare them to our own.

So let's heed Jesus' answer: "What is that to you? You must follow me." God's plans for my friend or neighbor are not his plans for me. It may be my calling to celebrate the evident grace or rich accomplishments in another person's life, while Christ calls me to a very different road. But the main thing is not whether our lives look like anyone else's, or even like our own plans and hopes would have them; the main thing is whether we are following Jesus.

⸺ ⸱ ⸺

John's Gospel ends there, but Matthew, Luke, and Acts (as well as the "long ending" of Mark) give us a view of what happens next: the ascension. We didn't visit any ascension sites on our tour, though we could see the traditional spot from a distance, as we looked back at the Mount of Olives from an overlook on Zion. One of the churches near that spot is the Russian Orthodox Church of the Ascension, and its tall belfry tower dominates the ridgeline of the Mount of Olives.

The ascension tends to get short shrift in much of western theology, overshadowed by the cross and empty tomb. We too often just use it as a simple explanation of why Jesus isn't physically here anymore, but this plays right into the suspicions of skeptics: how convenient that your Messiah, resurrected and immortal, just happened to disappear into the heavens rather than sticking around for people beyond his own circle to confirm it! But we understate the importance of the ascension if we think it's just a simple matter of Jesus going away. In early Christian theology, the ascension was the capstone of Jesus' passion: a fitting, meaningful, and crucial resolution to the story of the crucifixion and resurrection. In light of the way Old Testament patterns were fulfilled in Jesus' passion, the ascension is exactly what one should expect to happen after the resurrection.

The New Testament portrays Jesus' work on the cross in terms associated with Temple sacrifices, but crucially, it makes clear that Jesus is not only the sacrifice being offered, but the offerer as well (John 10:17-18; Heb. 7:27; 9:11–12). To Jews who had been raised within this system of religion, the claim that Jesus was the once-for-all sacrifice for sins would still strike them as an incomplete gospel. You don't just need a sacrifice, you also need someone who can bear that sacrifice on your behalf into the presence of God. So it would have made no sense for the story of Jesus' passion to end with the crucifixion and resurrection, because the presentation of the sacrifice was still incomplete. Sacrifices were made on the great altar outside the Temple doors, but that was only the first half of the ritual. There had to be a high priest who could complete the rite by taking the blood up into the Temple to present it before the Lord.

The idea of ascension into the presence of God was built into the very rituals of Temple worship: after the sacrifice was offered on the altar, the priest would take up some of the blood of the sacrifice, climb the steps up into the Temple itself, where clouds of incense in the Holy Place would hide him from the view of the worshipers outside, and then he would approach the Holy of Holies, the place where God's Shekinah glory dwelt. After presenting the blood of the sacrifice, the high priest would intercede for the people in the presence of the Lord, and then return to bestow God's blessings on the crowds outside.

This priestly drama is played out in the ascension. Jesus, our great High Priest, takes the sacrifice of himself and goes up into the true temple—the presence of God in heaven, beyond space or time—to present his sacrifice there. As he goes up, just as in the case of the high priest ascending into the smoke of the incense, a cloud hides him from the view of his disciples. And just as the high priest intercedes for the people while in the Temple, so also Jesus is interceding for us before the throne of the Father (Rom. 8:34). Further, in the same way that the high priest is expected to return to pronounce the blessings and judgments of God, so Jesus also will return one day. The language of the ascension in the New Testament is the language of the high priestly rite, hinted at in the Gospels and laid down clearly in Hebrews.

But that's not all. The ascension, just like Jesus clearing the Temple courts at the beginning of his passion week, is both a priestly and a kingly act. The other theme layered into the ascension accounts is that of the glorious vindication of the rightful king, raised up and enthroned in power beside God the Father. The image of Jesus being taken up into the clouds evokes not only priestly rites, but the great prophecy of the Son of Man in Daniel 7:13–14, who comes with the clouds of heaven, is led into the presence of the Ancient of Days, is granted power and authority, and receives the worship of the nations. This was one of the images of Jesus that was foremost in the early proclamations of the Jerusalem church. Jesus' ascension is the ultimate and indisputable declaration of his kingship, not only over Israel, but over all things.

This then, is the end of one story—the story of Jesus' earthly ministry—but, in the words of Augustine, it is no end. It is the beginning of Jesus' glorious heavenly ministry, reigning and interceding, and one day we will see our Priest-King return again, radiant in power and bearing salvation for all who believe.

Part 3

"Through the Church the Song Goes On"

Disciples, Saints, and Pilgrims

OF DOVES AND TONGUES OF FLAME

O, the outward hath gone!—but in glory and power,
The Spirit surviveth the things of an hour;
Unchanged, undecaying, its Pentecost flame
On the heart's secret altar is burning the same!

—John Greenleaf Whittier, "Palestine"

Our walk with Jesus doesn't end with the ascension. His work goes on, in and through us. The book of Acts, with its descriptions of the faith of the early church, show the continuance of Jesus' ministry through his followers. And so we still have a few more stories to tell, of places where our faithful forebears carried the message ever onward.

Let me take you back to the middle of my group's time in Jerusalem. As had happened on our first day in the city, we came to the end of our second day to find that we still had time remaining after seeing all the sites on our list. This was perfect: there was still another site nearby that I very much wanted to see, but which wasn't included on our initial agenda: the Cenacle, or, as it's better known to us, the Upper Room. One would think that the reputed site of both the Last Supper and Pentecost would be a must-see for most Christians, but it gets left off tour schedules for three reasons: (1) because its authenticity is questioned; (2) because it's a disputed area caught amid the tensions of Christianity, Islam, and Judaism; and (3) because there's frankly not much to see there—it's one of the rare instances in which a modern site actually might look quite a bit like the original: just a big, plain, open room.

But I had done some advance reading on the site, and I found the historical case for its authenticity to be, if not compelling, at least plausible. There is a very ancient thread of evidence, going back to traditions associated with the early Jewish-Christian community in that spot, which pointed to this location as the Upper Room of Jesus and the apostles. So, with extra time on our hands, we made our way to the Cenacle.

Though the Upper Room is a holy site associated with only one of the three major religions, it's in the unfortunate situation of sitting directly on top of another site with a far more dubious claim: the reputed "Tomb of David" (though virtually all scholars now agree that this late tradition is almost certainly false, and David is buried elsewhere). But the ascription is enough to make both Jews and Muslims claim a religious interest in the site. The Upper Room, for its part, has gone through many back-and-forth periods in which it was a Christian church or a Muslim mosque. This explains the fact why no religious enhancement of the site has taken place for some time; it remains an empty room, with an armed guard stationed not far away. Nonetheless, the fantastic importance of the place was enough to suffuse it with wonder for me.

As we approached the Cenacle, along a raised walkway that joined two sections of the larger building, we could hear the sound of Pentecostal worship bursting out from within. Sure enough, there was a large group of Pentecostal Christians there, shouting and singing and speaking in tongues in the wild, joyful revelry of being in the place where the Holy Spirit was first poured out on the infant church. It didn't bother me—I rather like Pentecostals, and what better place for them to be at their high tide of Pentacostal-ishness than in the Upper Room?

Since the interior was occupied by a chanting mob, we paused outside the open doorway to do our little service of prayer out there. And this is where one of the weirdly fantastical events of our Israel trip occurred. I've already narrated a few times in which I felt like God was using the birds of Israel to bless or encourage me in various ways—in most of those stories, it was a subjective experience that was only relevant to me. But this time, I'm pretty sure some of my tour-mates noticed it too. You will recall, of course, that the dove is used as the symbol of the Holy Spirit, both in artwork and in the Bible, and that the Upper Room was the very place where the Holy Spirit had been poured out in miraculous fashion. Well, (and I swear I'm not making this up), as we stood there doing our service on the threshold of the Upper Room, a dove swooped down right over our heads, flew straight into the open doorway of the Upper Room, and then out the doorway on the other side. Was it mere coincidence, or a sign of God's wild and winsome grace, that the symbol of the Holy Spirit should be soaring right over our heads at the scene of Pentecost? I'm inclined to account it the latter.

———·———

My undergraduate training was in linguistics, so the story of Pentecost has always fascinated me, particularly the miracle of xenolalia—the disciples being heard in all the different languages of their audience. This story, told in Acts 2, is a reversal of the tragedy of the Tower of Babel (Gen. 11). With the New Creation inaugurated in Christ, the curse of the fall is being undone in the community of the church. Whereas the multiplicity of languages pushed people apart in those early days of pride and pomp, now God was turning the tables and using languages to bring people together into the united covenant-community of Jesus.

This miracle of languages was also a sign of God's intention to redeem people from all lands, all nations, all ethnic groups. The first generation of Christians realized very quickly that the gospel of Jesus Christ was not limited to Jews, nor even to the Greek God-fearers who pressed into their synagogues.

It was a message for all peoples under the sun, as foretold throughout the pages of Scripture.

One of the great passions of my life, and one of the great delights of my service, has been my involvement in this grand narrative of bringing the message of Christ to all nations. Raised in a missionary family, we were very conscious of this onward-rolling history of the proclamation of the gospel to those who had never before heard it. We knew that we were part of a great legacy of stepping out to carry God's love for all nations to its ultimate conclusion, when people from every nation, tribe, people, and tongue would worship around the throne of God (Rev. 7:9). Our forefathers had come to the faith through the work of missionaries many centuries before; now we had the honor of bearing the flame to other lands and laboring beside the new missionaries God was raising up from those very places. This grand, unstoppable story has been going on since the moment of Pentecost, and we stand now on the threshold of seeing its first great fulfillment within our lifetimes.

Consider this: never before in the history of Christianity—not for two thousand years—has the message of Christ been available to every people group in the world. There have always been ethnic groups in isolated areas, or in countries closed to the gospel because of religious or political hostility, which have never been exposed to the message of Christianity. There are still many such groups today, but now, for the first time, we are within sight of the first great milestone on this journey of serving the mission of God. Some mission agencies are predicting that within five years, every people group in the entire world will have a witness for Jesus present in their midst. That has never happened before, not in all the ages of Christian history. But it's happening right now, thanks to the committed work of local missionaries, of indigenous disciple-making movements, and of revivals sweeping through even the most hostile corners of the earth.

We are living in the dawning fulfillment of the promise made to Abraham four thousand years ago—that every people group on earth would be blessed through his faith, summed up in Christ (Gen. 12:3). This is a staggering realization. We are living in the very age that many great women and men of God longed to see, and yet they did not see it. We twenty-first century Christians will get to see and celebrate a milestone that the greatest missionaries from all ages—from Paul to Patrick to William Carey to Amy Carmichael— yearned for with their whole lives. So let's not miss the importance of this moment, nor delay it any longer by remaining aloof or unprayerful while the harvest is being gathered in.

There will still be a great deal of work to come, of course—just having a living witness in every group is not enough, and in some places the population of unbelievers is growing faster than the spread of the Christian message. Further, there will always remain the hard, beautiful labor of pouring out the blessings of God's kingdom over all peoples and nations. We will carry on the precious works of healing, education, development, and peacemaking everywhere we go. But even as those tasks persist, sometimes amid monumental challenges, we should not underestimate the dramatic importance of this moment, when there will be, for the very first time ever, members of the Body of Christ who come from every tribe, tongue, people, and nation. The proclamation to the nations at Pentecost is still sweeping across nations like wildfire today, and we are a part of its story.

———·———

We took a few minutes to slip into the Cenacle itself, looking around while the Pentecostal group continued their worship. It was wide and plain, but showed evidence of its previous use: the pillars and simple Gothic vaulting remained a testimony of its Crusader heritage (along with a beautiful capital illustrating a Christian bird-symbol: the legend of the self-sacrificing pelican, a common medieval sign for Christ), as well as the qibla-niche and Arabic calligraphy that attested to its later use as a mosque.

I tried to imagine Jesus there with his disciples, talking and eating together: the wonder and holiness of that moment, of the King of the Universe kneeling to wash dirt-caked feet, of the loaf and the grail, of Jesus' giving his great new commandment: "Love one another as I have loved you." But the room was full of boisterous praise, not of stillness, and my mind was drawn toward another day, of the Spirit's fire and tongues and preaching, and of a day yet further down the road: the great eruption of celebration and praise at the final "last supper," when we feast again with our Lord, together with people from every tribe and nation, in the kingdom that is to come.

ZION'S HOPE FULFILLED

One privilege my heart desires:
O grant me an abode
Among the churches of Thy saints,
The temples of my God!

—Isaac Watts, "The Lord of Glory Is My Light" (Ps. 27)

O n one day of our trip, our travels took us out of the West
Bank and back toward Jerusalem. That drive highlighted
once again the harsh realities of life in certain areas of this divided
country. Walls, guns, and checkpoints—it was a stark reminder
that there, in the land of the Prince of Peace himself, we still
awaited with heartbroken longing the final consummation of his
kingdom.

This time, we stopped in a different area of Jerusalem: a corner just beyond the southwest walls of the Old City, at an overlook that gazed over the City of David and the Mount of Olives

on one side, and down into the Hinnom Valley (biblical "Gehenna") on the other side. In the trees nearby, Eurasian Blackcaps feasted on fruit trees, and Rose-ringed Parakeets flashed across our sight.

We were standing now in the part of the city that had been the center of the early church. For the past two thousand years, it had been known as Zion. Now, I've already confessed to one topographical surprise that hit me in the Holy Land—the way the Temple faced—but here was another one. Zion wasn't actually where I thought it should be. The thoughtful reader might have already noticed that I'm using that name to refer to a section of Jerusalem that is not the Temple Mount. And that might strike some as odd, since much of the Old Testament seems to have the Temple Mount in mind when it speaks of Zion.

It turns out that the name has shifted throughout time, having been adopted for the most prominent sections of town throughout Jerusalem's history. "Zion" probably first referred to the ridge on which the most ancient portion of the city sat—the southeasterly City of David, and then after the construction of the Temple the name was shifted north to coincide with Mount Moriah, the site of the Temple. Oddly, though, sometime around the turning of millennia from BC to AD, Jews began referring to the southwestern hill of Jerusalem—not the Temple Mount—as Zion. Some scholars think that this happened because part of that area of town happened to be very wealthy, as well as maintaining a high religious significance (many priests lived there). Because of this high profile, its residents flattered themselves by referring to their home district with the ancient and venerable name of Zion. Thus, by the time Jesus and the disciples were tromping around Jerusalem, Zion was no longer consistently applied to the Temple Mount, but to the hill that lay in the southwestern quarter of the city.

By this time you're surely looking for something more interesting to read, but bear with me a bit longer. This geographical tangent is important for the Christian story of Jerusalem. Why? Well, it just so happens that it was that very southwestern hill, the "Mount Zion" of the first century AD, where the church itself began. It was on the hill of Zion that Jesus and his disciples met in the Upper Room for the Last Supper; it was on the hill of Zion that Christ stood trial before the high priest; it was on the hill of Zion that the resurrected Jesus appeared to his disciples again; and it was on the hill of Zion that the Holy Spirit was poured out at Pentecost.

For the entire first generation of the early church, Zion was the epicenter of the Christian movement: it was there that the early members of the Jerusalem church gathered together; there that the first great church council was held (Acts 15); there that James exercised his pastoral office; and there that later generations of Christians pointed to as the home community of Jewish Christianity. By the Byzantine era, there was a massive basilica on the spot, the Church of Hagia Sion ("Holy Zion"), marking and celebrating the birthplace of the faith.

So, by a strange (or providential?) turn of history, "Zion" just happened to be the name of the district of Jerusalem where the church began. In this light, when we read the many spectacular sayings of the Old Testament in regard to Mount Zion, they suddenly take on a new shade of meaning: a prophetic air, pointing to Jesus and the church. Now those verses don't merely depict the glory of God's presence in the Temple, they foreshadow what God was going to do on the southwestern hill of Jerusalem in the age of the Messiah. When we read "Oh, that salvation for Israel would come out of Zion!" (Ps. 53:6), how can we not think of the salvation poured out upon the newborn church there? When we hear Isaiah say, "See, I lay a stone in Zion, a tested stone, a precious cornerstone on a firm foundation" (Is. 28:16), how can we not be reminded of Jesus? As in many cases throughout the Old Testament, it appears that God has been erecting signposts pointing toward the great works of grace to come.

———·———

We trudged a bit further up the slope of Mount Zion, past the Zion Gate of the Old City and into a remarkably narrow alley that led to the precincts where the ancient Byzantine cathedral of Hagia Sion once stood. Today a beautiful Christian church stands once again on Zion—the Dormition Abbey, constructed by German Catholics in the late nineteenth century. The present church is built in honor of the tradition that the Virgin Mary lived out her years there, and that it was there that she fell asleep in the Lord (to use the original Christian way of talking about death).

There are other churches on Zion today, for it's the same hill where Caiaphas' house sits, as well as the Upper Room. Where Jesus' accusers had called that hill "Zion" in an apparent act of pride, Jesus would make it the truest of Zions by the unbounded grace of salvation through his name. Jesus turned the tables of human arrogance on their head, remaking history in such a dramatic way that even the antagonistic philosopher Friedrich Nietzsche called it "the transvaluation of all values." Jesus had turned his place of trial and anguish into the very place where new life would be poured out: for there on Zion, just up the hill from the high priest's dungeon-pit, stood the Upper Room, and the shadow of Jesus' tortures was to be lit by the joyful fire of Pentecost's flames.

SEEING THROUGH
THE KINGFISHER'S EYES

We turn aside and tread the ways
That lead through wonder up to praise.

—Henry van Dyke, "The Burning Bush"

The story of the apostolic church pours out through the streets of Zion, beyond Jerusalem, and across the roads of the Roman Empire. Many of those roads led through a port city called Caesarea Maritima, the main hub for Palestine's seagoing traffic. With all the comings and goings of the apostolic generation to which the city played witness, it appears often in the book of Acts, most prominently as the place where Peter met with Cornelius and the Gentiles were first accepted into the Christian faith, and later where Paul was imprisoned before being sent on to Rome. After the first century, over the course of the next few hundred years, Caesarea Maritima would go on to become a major center of Christian faith and learning, a home to famous martyrs, theologians, and church historians.

———.———

Our drive to Caesarea, on the Mediterranean coast, was relatively short, but the beauties of the land made it seem full of splendors. I saw birds along the way, of course—a few fleeting glimpses that I couldn't place, and a few others that I recognized from my hours of field guide study: mostly White-spectacled Bulbuls winging their loose and floppy flight from bush to bush. But it was the flowers that really stood out. I had often seen pictures of the Holy Land looking bare and dried-out (a common experience, I think; one of my parishioners begged me before I left, "Please, see if you can take just one picture of something green in Israel!"). Yet here was an avalanche of color bursting out on every side. The week before we had arrived, they had received the blessing of rain—even rain that penetrated into the Judean desert beyond the hills. And everywhere, Norah told us, wildflowers were bursting into bloom.

Our first stop in Caesarea was at a site just a bit removed from the ancient city—the remnants of an old aqueduct running near the beach. Here was another of King Herod's great constructions. Despite his much-deserved reputation as a villain of biblical history, one cannot help marveling at his accomplishments, whose architectural achievements even won admiration from his imperial overlords in Rome. And the aqueduct before us, though one of the least of his creations, was nonetheless impressive: a monumental structure of which long stretches still remained intact, and which achieved the herculean feat of bringing fresh water all the way from the distant highlands to the saltwater lowlands of the Caesarean coast.

As marvelous as the ingenious creations of man's mind are, however, my attention was caught by something even more breathtaking: a living wonder of God's work. As I gazed out over the waves of the sea, I noticed an odd black-and-white shape hovering over a distant inlet. At first I thought it was a kite floating on the wind, but then it folded its wings and struck down like a dart into the water. It took me a few moments to make sense of what I was seeing, but as the bird rose again, hovered, and then dove a second time, I realized that it was a Pied Kingfisher: a boldly-emblazoned, zebra-toned bird that could pause motionless in the sky and then whirl down like a thunderbolt.

———.———

My visit to Caesarea was, for me, an opportunity to step through the doorway of history in a new and powerful way. The main thrust of my scholarly work is church history, and Caesarea is where the discipline was born. Of course, one might make the case that Luke was really the first church historian; but the man who first attempted the vast, synthesizing, sense-making work of church history in a substantial and lasting way was Eusebius of Caesarea, who lived in that city in the early fourth century. I had often felt a special connection to Eusebius—not only as a scholar of church history, but as a man who had served as a pastor at the same time, just as I did. I had read through his famous tome, the *Ecclesiastical History,* in the process of doing an independent research project in seminary—one of the times in my life when I felt most fully the joy of being a scholar.

But what's so fascinating about church history? My contention, by way of a bird metaphor, is that it lets you see through the kingfisher's eyes. The Pied kingfisher had the ability to stop, suspended in the air for a moment, hovering there as if freezing out all distractions, and look down to see exactly where its target was. In the same way, it can be a very valuable thing to have a glimpse at an issue in a way that freezes out all the other distractions of our contemporary world. Church history does that for us. It enables us to look at a point of theology, a Christian practice, or the interpretation of a Bible verse while wearing the lenses of another age, rather than our own.

C. S. Lewis, in his introduction to Athanasius' *On the Incarnation,* makes the case that we need to peer through the lenses of church history (specifically, by reading the great old books that those from previous eras have left us) in order to avoid the "characteristic blindness" of our own age. We carry implicit cultural blind spots that we aren't even aware of, and they can affect how we think, act, and yes, even how we read the Bible. But studying church history, and seeing the way that the Holy Spirit worked through women and men of a different age, with different blind spots than our own, can be an illuminating exercise. They think about the world in ways that would never occur to us, and they can often see things in the text of Scripture that we have missed, though we have read those passages a hundred times.

One of my seminary professors described studying church history as being akin to having our youth groups go on short-term mission trips. One of the blessings of those experiences, over and above the practical work that gets done for the sake of the kingdom, is that those young people are shaken out of their cultural blinders, even if just for a moment, and asked to see the world in a whole new way.

Of course, the books that are left to us by earlier ages have their own blind spots, too—Eusebius is sometimes criticized for being too sympathetic to heretical Arians, or of being a political yes-man for Emperor Constantine. He, like all of us, was a man of his time, and he had his own blind spots. But the great value of walking a few roads with him is that his blind spots are not the same as ours, and so his voice, together with all the giants of the patristic age, can help wake us up to a new, brighter, and fuller picture of the faith that God has given us.

———·———

A few minutes later we pulled up to the national park that enshrined the ruins of Caesarea. We emerged from the ticket line into the plaza at the center of Caesarea's ruins, fringed by flowers and statuary, and opening onto the vista of the ancient harbor. Stretching out before us was a short promontory arrayed in pillars and blocks, and now swarmed with bright-shirted tourists from a dozen different countries. There stood the remains of Herod's palace. Away to the right was the curving arc of the harbor, lined with long, flat stretches that called to mind a broad avenue or the course of a hippodrome. And there, at the far end, was a longer promontory stretching out into the sea, a piece of the old artificial harbor that had made Caesarea Maritima one of the architectural marvels of its age: the construction, out of sheer ingenuity and skill, of a world-class harbor along a notoriously harborless coast.

But we didn't explore any of these areas at first. Our first item of business, here as everywhere, was to pause and have our little mini-service of worship, Scripture, and prayer. And so we stepped through some flowers to a nearby set of flat ruins, a bit out of the way of the main flow of traffic. As soon as I saw the spot we had picked, I knew what it was. We were standing in a church. Though only partial sections of lowest set of blocks remained of the walls, it was still possible to make out the shape of the little nave and the rounded apse, and of a sacristy beyond. There were even partial mosaics underneath our feet, preserved over more than a millennium and a half. It was a small church, but its simple shape and artwork pointed all the way back to the Byzantine era, when the old Roman Empire had become Christian. Though small, it must have been a church of some importance, standing as it did in the very heart of the harbor district.

I immediately felt a deep sense of connection, once again, with this land. The reminders that this was the homeland of my faith were everywhere, even where I did not expect to find them. I already knew the biblical connections with these places—this was the spot where Peter had met Cornelius, and thus where the Gentiles first received the Gospel; and this was also one of the many locations of Paul's imprisonments—but for me, for whom church history had always been a powerful and precious part of my life, this moment of connection with the church through the ages was quietly profound. I thought of the great scholars of the early church who had walked these very places, lived within these streets, and perhaps prayed in this very spot: Origen, Pamphilius, and Eusebius, among many others. It pleased me immensely to be standing in a spot where Eusebius had likely stood—more than that, where he may have prayed and served as a minister. While the others in the group were still shuffling about into their places, I stole a moment to bend down, touch the dusty mosaics, and breathe a prayer that God might inspire and use my thoughts and writings to bless others in just a fraction of the way that he had used Eusebius.

The rest of Caesarea was fascinating, though only fragmentary ruins remained. The most impressive feature is the ancient amphitheater, now rebuilt as a modern concert venue. But there were other points of interest, too, like the swimming-pools Herod had built out into the Mediterranean surf, still visible today. Gracing the fringes of these ruins were two brilliant, elegant egrets, hunting fish among the rippling waves. Once again, the wonders of man's ingenuity had fallen into ruin, while the Creator's wonders remained marvels in every age.

IN THE HALLS OF MY HEROES

Kneeling in prayer, and not ashamed to pray,
The tumult of the time disconsolate
To inarticulate murmurs dies away,
While the eternal ages watch and wait.

—Henry Wadsworth Longfellow,
"Three Sonnets on the Divina Commedia"

A s we follow the story of the Christian faith out of the pages
of Scripture and into the annals of history, I have one last
story to tell. Of course, there are many stories in Israel about the
great heroes of the faith who lived or visited there, from John
Damascene writing in his monastery to D. L. Moody preaching sermons outside Jerusalem's walls. But for the last tale of my
pilgrimage, I want to take you back to those particular heroes who

so captured my mind as a young man—the desert fathers, monks who lived out an ascetic faith in the barren wilderness beyond the hills.

———·———

The arid ravines of the West Bank still look today much as they had looked when Christian holy men wandered their wastes back in Byzantine days. Our route took us down through those hills and then into the valley of the Dead Sea, far below sea level. I was excited for this excursion, for we were finally going to see just a bit of the old Israel that I had studied so fiercely: the home of those long-gone ascetics, the abbas and ammas, who shook the nations with their prayers from those very wilderness slopes. The Judean desert, along with Egypt and Syria, had once been at the center of a movement of piety and prayer that transformed Christian practice across the world.

We followed a road that traced the ancient highway between Jerusalem and Jericho, and Najji pulled the bus over next to a sun-bleached hill with a large cross mounted on top. As we went from air-conditioned comfort into the full light of day, it felt as if we were stepping into a blast furnace. From the crest, we looked out over a desolate landscape of stony, dusty rises and land so hard-baked by the sun that it was hard to believe Norah's story about a rare rain making the place bloom just days before. The main object of attraction, though, was down in the valley below us: a monastery that clung to the cliff like an ibex, with old trails leading to the rocky caves where hermits had labored in prayer fifteen centuries before. Most Protestant pilgrimage groups who stop here are interested in the old tradition that identifies this spot as "the valley of the shadow of death" referenced in Psalm 23, and it certainly looked like it could have been a dangerous passage back in the days of highway brigandage.

But my interest was locked on the monastery itself. This was St. George's Monastery, named after George the Chozebite, one of its most famous residents. I would have most loved to see the famous Mar Saba monastery, just a few miles away, but St. George's was a satisfying consolation prize. Still, I felt a twinge of regret that I was this close, and yet would not at any point get to step within the halls of my heroes—I could only look at them from afar.

The monastery clung to a spot in Wadi Qelt that had long been associated with Elijah's wilderness flight, when God had sent ravens to bring food to the lonely, anguished prophet on the run. As it happened, while we drove away from the overlook site, I spotted a species of raven I had never seen before, one that specialized in just those desert environments: the Brown-necked Raven of Israel's wastes, and Elijah's old companion.

After a brief stop for a photo-op with a local camel, we plunged down into the bleakest wasteland of all: the Dead Sea basin. It looked like a whole different world. There was more color here than in the hills of the Judean desert—the russet brown of the cliffs, the blue saltwater, the vanishingly tiny fringe of verdure here and there around its edge, the red and black mountains of Moab on the other side, and over all of it a shimmering veil of haze. We had seen a bit of this landscape at Qumran, but now we would see all of it, as we drove the length of the sea from north to south. But before we did, we were going to partake in one of the peculiar rites of passage for all tourists to Israel: a dip in the salty sea itself. So there, amid waves of heat that turned the sand into a scalding oven floor, we rushed down to the beach and, for a few minutes, indulged in the weird thrill of bobbing in the water. 'Water' is perhaps too generous a term, though—it had a silty, faintly slimly quality to it, that clung to one's skin in odd and unnerving ways.

Masada was our destination, the old mountaintop fortress that Herod had crafted as his desert showpiece. It held a special place in my imagination. I had first encountered the story of Masada as a teenager, when I was doing research for my first novel, set in the Jewish revolt of AD 70. That war had ended with one last, suicidal stand by the brave Jewish rebels who had holed themselves up in this remote mountain palace and held out for years while the Roman army besieged them. In the end, the final defenders opted to take their own lives rather than fall to the Romans' blades, and the account of their final stand was etched into my memory. (I had even modeled the site of one of the battles in my fantasy epic, *Freedom Cry*, on Masada.) I was far from the only one captivated by the story of Masada's fall; even the Israeli army would often bring its new soldiers-in-training there to be inspired by the desperate heroism of those last brave rebels.

After its destruction by the Romans, the location of Masada had been forgotten by the ages. So steep were its slopes and so isolated were its ruins that it wasn't until Europeans began exploring the area in the nineteenth century that it was rediscovered (or so I was told). Nowadays, thankfully, one need not climb the rugged escarpment up to the mountaintop (though there is a trail available for that if you so choose); a modern cable car glides you gracefully up to the summit. Norah took us on an extended tour of the

fortress-palace's grounds, many walls of which still remained at least partially in place. We saw the grand sweep of the old Herodian palace, complete
with cistern water-systems, bathhouses, and a three-tiered balcony palisade;
and we stood in the room where the last Jewish defenders drew their lots to
decide who would deal the final blows in their mass suicide. One of the most
remarkable things was that one could still see, in clear outlines on the valley
floor below, each of the Roman army encampments from the siege they had
lain two millennia before.

All the while, of course, I was keeping an eye out for the varied and
ever-present bird life. It was something of an astonishment to see how many
species called that desolate wasteland their home and seemed to make a good
living of it there: more of the beautiful Tristram's Starlings, along with Fan-
tailed Ravens, Crag Martins, and Short-toed Snake Eagles, to say nothing of
the ubiquitous House Sparrows, which not even the most ungodly furnace in
the world can restrain. There in that tragic place, where the Jewish homeland
met its most heart-rending dissolution; there where the sin-scapes of Sodom
and Gomorrah lay sunken in the ancient basin of death; there where the
vast armies of Moab and Ammon had been cut low in a bloody, self-inflicted
massacre in King Jehoshaphat's day—there the beauty of God's creation still
spoke the loudest word, and above the sea of death there was life, majestic,
soaring on the wind.

Despite all that I knew about Masada even before arriving there, it still
had one delicious final surprise for me. As we finished up the tour, Norah
turned to us and asked, "Would anyone like to see the church?" Not giving
a moment for any of my heat-stricken, footsore fellow pilgrims to respond, I
immediately jumped in and said yes, and she brought us to a tiny chapel that
sat in the vast open space in the middle of Masada. Its walls were largely intact,
though without a roof, and in a side-room there was a beautiful mosaic laid
out on the floor. The curve of the apse, which looked out over the vista of the
Dead Sea, spoke in no uncertain terms that this was a church. "Oh yes," Norah
told us, "some Byzantine monks had a little monastery up here for a while!"

I smiled at the irony—despite the pretensions of European explorers, it
had not been they who first rediscovered the lost palaces of Masada; it had
been the wandering desert fathers of old Byzantium, many centuries before.
After I returned home, I did a little research and found that the monastery
there had been called Marda, and that it had carried on with between twelve

and twenty monks for most of the fifth century; and that, further, it had been founded by perhaps the most intrepid desert father of all: Euthymius the Great, to whom the monastic movement in Palestine owed much for his inspiring example and leadership.

So there, on the very day that I had lamented that I would not get the chance to step into one of the monasteries of my ancient heroes, God gave me the surprise of letting me do just that. I stooped down and touched the dusty ground, where Euthymius and his brothers had sung and prayed so long ago, and I thanked God that he had granted me the chance to walk in the same daring footsteps they had left behind: to leave off the world's temptations and live as a lighthouse of prayer, a city on a hill that cannot be hidden.

THE ROAD HOME,
AND ONWARD

Blest land of Judea! thrice hallowed of song,
Where the holiest of memories pilgrim-like throng;
In the shade of thy palms, by the shores of thy sea,
On the hills of thy beauty, my heart is with thee.

—John Greenleaf Whittier, "Palestine"

Our time in Israel had drawn to a close. We had a final farewell
dinner at our hotel, and then it was back to Ben Gurion airport, where we waited bleary-eyed for our midnight flight back
to Boston. The travels back home went by in something of a blur;
I don't remember much of it at all—not the flight, nor the bus
ride from Boston up into Maine, nor my long drive from the bus
station back to my own hometown. But I do remember the joy
of coming home, of seeing my wife and kids again, whom I had

missed deeply, in a way that I hadn't quite realized until that very moment. And then, as I recall, I immediately went to bed and slept for fourteen hours.

My pilgrimage to the Holy Land had been a wonderful experience: in many ways, it had far exceeded even the highest expectations I had for it, giving me many surprising works of grace along the way. My birding goals had also been met and surpassed in significant measure, as I racked up nearly four times as many sightings as I had dared to hope for. But the sweetest thing of all, of course, was the spiritual joy I had found in more than one of my adventures in the Holy Land. For months thereafter, the memory of Israel (and Galilee in particular) exercised a strange gravity on me. It kept coming back to my mind, in all the in-between moments, with a fond, peaceful longing, as in Longfellow's reminiscence of his boyhood home: "And the friendships old and the early loves / Come back with a Sabbath sound, as of doves / In quiet neighborhoods." It was Israel's "Sabbath sound, as of doves" that I kept hearing in my heart, as the journey I had walked with Jesus there began to mold the shape of my journeys yet to come.

But it wasn't until after I came back home that I began to realize that something had happened to me in Israel. I had gone there longing for transformation, for a taste of long-sought holiness, and I had hoped that it might come for me as it had for Mary of Egypt in ancient days: a blazing moment of sanctification run wild. Now I was slowly discovering, day by day, that something was different in me, but it wasn't as if a new, unforeseen work of grace had been sealed and accomplished there across the sea; it was more like the realization that the hidden seed of some mighty thing to come had been planted quietly in my heart, and I was beginning to see the first gentle blade of verdure break the soil.

There were several distinct ways in which I came to notice that a new growth had begun. I wasn't expecting it, to be honest. My days in Israel had come and gone without any kind of clear transformation-experience, so I was expecting the same old stumbles when it came to re-entering my daily life. Nothing led me to believe that my nagging little wrestlings with the simplest of temptations would ever go away. But after a few weeks, I realized with some astonishment that I was suddenly doing a good deal better in most of the areas I had been working on: temptations seemed easier to brush off, virtue fit more naturally as my customary habit of life, and taking up my spiritual disciplines felt as natural as putting on my slippers. The feeling has faded somewhat since then, and some old battles are still battles, but those months after Israel remain a sweet reminder to me that the pilgrimage continues, and that the homeland that I long to find is a very real destination.

But there was even more growth to come: growth that not only encouraged my desires, but helped me re-orient my perspective on them. I came under the conviction that even my very quest for holiness called for some watchfulness. It carried with it a danger of misdirected motives, the trap of being driven by discontentedness with myself more than by the delight of pursuing God. And little by little, I began to understand something I had never understood before: I started to get a sense of why God never seemed to want to answer my prayers for immediate deliverance and bursts of sanctification. It wasn't that God was being cruel, choosing to ignore me despite his power to help (though that was what I had assumed in some of the doldrums of my spiritual life). No, it was that God was offering me something better the whole time. In place of an instantaneous deliverance that would paper over the surface of my troubles, he wanted to lead me on a journey of uncovering deeper wounds, ones that I had not even really been aware of, but whose pain was nonetheless pulling my heart in this endless round of high hopes and frustrated failings. In his great love, he was offering me a healing far deeper than I had imagined.

One experience in particular stands out for me, amid all the blessings of those months after my pilgrimage. I was at home, reading a passage from one of my favorite books, Julian of Norwich's *Revelations of Divine Love,* when all of the sudden I had an image spring into my mind. It was Jesus, sitting on a rock in the shade of a tree, and I knew at once that we were back again in Galilee. And as I looked at him, and he at me, I could feel his wordless invitation pulsating through my soul. I stepped close to him, and he reached out, took my head in his hands, as one would do to a beloved child, and then held my head to his chest. It was a breathlessly intimate moment of radical acceptance. That was all there was to the image, but it was so powerful in all its silent, infinite understanding, that it drove me to my knees.

That single experience, more than any treatises ever penned, reminded me of the great truth of God's love. He could look at me—the same "me" that I saw with disgruntled disaffection, riddled with petty inconsistencies in my lukewarm attempts to live as a dedicated Christian—and he loved that very "me"—yes, as hard as it is to believe, he loved me! I would need to find ways to love myself, including the self that I very much did not always love, because that was precisely who Jesus loved.

Author Christine Pohl notes that we, at times, choose to give our attention to what we think is an ideal, even if it does not really exist, rather than learning to embrace the "real" that is right in front of us. When we do this in our sexuality, we call it pornography. So what should we call it when we obsessively pursue an unreal ideal of our own spiritual self? Spiritual pornography, perhaps. Is that what I was guilty of in my longings for holiness? Maybe, at least a little bit. Some of my desire sprang from a distinct yearning to be closer to God, and some of it was the agony of having to live with the darts of sin striking around me…but there was a large part of it, too, that was simply a sense of discontentment with myself. I had to be careful not to make the ideal of a hoped-for, future, saintly self into an idol. Holiness is our birthright and our calling in Christ, but we will not inherit its fullness by being anything other than our authentic selves. One of the many things Israel taught me was that I needed to rest in Jesus' love, and to start giving thanks for who I already was, before I could heal unto holiness.

The medieval writer Bernard of Clairvaux, in his book *On the Love of God,* writes that there are four levels of love that one can attain. The simplest love, sometimes indistinguishable from selfishness or pride, is to love oneself for one's own sake. The second level, as experienced by many new converts, is to love God for one's own sake (i.e., for the consolations of joy, peace, and hope that one feels in relationship with God). The third level, and the one that most people think would probably be the highest, is to love God for God's own sake—captivated by his glory. But Bernard puts one level higher even than that: the fourth and highest level of love, he says, is to learn to love oneself for God's sake. And that, my friends, is the pilgrimage I am on.

~ The End ~

The Blackbird and the Praying Saint

Before he came to Glendalough,
Before his bed of stone gave rest,
Saint Kevin was a Cornwall monk,
And learned from Saint Petroc the bless'd.

Some men are fashioned for the crowd,
For hearty smiles and time with friends;
But Kevin, no, not one of these:
His were the mountains and the glens.

The company of saints and monks
Would be his calling and his kin;
But in his heart he longed to be
Among the wilds and the wind.

And so he took much time alone
Amid the hours in abbey walls,
To play the hermit on the hill,
Where skylark soars and blackbird calls.

One Lententide he prayed up there,
All by himself, but not alone;
For with him all creation prayed
Where river ran and sunlight shone.

He prayed with mind and with his mouth,
His heart confessed its sinful dross;
And with his body too he prayed,
His arms outstretched in holy cross.

Then on his palm he felt the touch
Of tiny feet and tiny claws;
He saw a blackbird roosting there,
And in its beak a clutch of straws.

It fashioned in his outstretched hand
A nest for raising up its chicks;
And there it settled, all at peace,
Within its bowl of straw and sticks.

Saint Kevin held the nest aloft
In sacred reverence of its load;
And he with bird, in patience prayed
Above the monastery road.

The eggs were laid, and still he stood
Like Moses o'er the battle fray,
And angels were his Aaron, Hur,
Upholding arms stretched out to pray.

Day after day he stood there, still,
While eggs were hatched inside the nest;
And chicks were fledged, and stood, and flew,
Before Saint Kevin earned his rest.

The legend says he stood in prayer
Till mother bird had gone her way;
Her nest had stood on his sure branch
All through that Lent, to Easter day.

Sometimes in life we are the bird,
And need a place of peace to rest;
So fly unto the holy cross,
And there alone construct your nest.

The cross will hold you, it is sure,
For it is fixed in God's great love;
And at the cross you are upheld
By Christ himself, who reigns above.

And sometimes too we are the saint,
Called to stand and wait in prayer;
So be the blessing this world needs,
Be Saint Kevin, if you dare:

Your prayers, your love, can be the tool
To grant your neighbors peace from strife;
So persevere in loving prayer,
And bring the blessing through to life.

(A poem about the Celtic monk Kevin of Glendalough, as mentioned in the Part 2 chapter on Nazareth: "I Cried Out, and He Answered Me")

ABOUT THE AUTHOR

Matthew Burden is an ordained minister of the American Baptist Churches, and he serves as pastor of a church in eastern Maine, where he lives with his wife and three children. He is the author of several novels and works of poetry, with an upcoming book on the theology of Christian identity, *Who We Were Meant to Be*, set to be released soon. He holds graduate degrees in divinity and history, and is currently engaged in earning a PhD in theology, focusing on issues of historical missiology. Among his interests are church history, dusty old books, birding, and maintaining a whimsical disdain for the pace of modern life.

Website/Blog: thepeaceandthepassion.blogspot.com
(with daily posts featuring original essays, poems,
hymns, and photography)

Twitter & Instagram: @matthewburden05

OTHER BOOKS BY MATTHEW BURDEN

The Hidden Kings Trilogy:
Freedom Cry
The Conqueror's Song
Pathways of Mercy

Whispers of Adventure: A New Pilgrim's Progress for Today's Christian

Thus Ends the World, and Other Poems